MW01241272

Be sure to check out the chapter of deliverance.

Not Forsaking

Dr. E. C. Fulcher, Jr.

Published by
Dr. E. C. Fulcher, Jr.

Warning! Warning! Warning!

Hopefully, you will read the whole book because it is essential to your faith and eternal experience.

All scriptures referred to in this book are from the King James Version unless otherwise indicated.

Dr Fulcher modeled this book's numbering after Robert Estienne (Robert Stephanus), who was the first to number the verses within each chapter of the Bible, his verse numbers entering printed editions in 1551.

For more information about this ministry, visit our website at www.truthhouse.org or www.thvbn.tv

DR. FULCHER IS COVERING THE WORLD WITH SHORT-WAVE RADIO. VISIT OUR WEBSITE FOR RADIO FREQUENCY AND TIMES!

You can write to Dr. Fulcher using the address below:

Dr. E. C. Fulcher, Jr.
Po Box 973
Abingdon, Md. 21009

The Ministry of Dr. E. C. Fulcher, Jr.

The man of God grew up against an ecclesiastical tapestry of brotherly love and people's rights. His dad was a Pentecostal preacher whom Pastor recognized as doctrinally misguided and confused at an early age. In fact, all the preachers he met, and there were many, suffered from the same affliction.

Inspired by the truths of God's word (which, one by one, God revealed to him in his early ministry), Dr. Fulcher became increasingly aware of God's promise that he would someday lead the strongest church in history. In this vision, Dr. Fulcher saw a church that would no longer see through a glass darkly and would be doctrinally perfect (without spot or blemish) to be the bride of Christ, just as the Bible prophesied.

In his own words, six distinguishing messages define his ministry:
*   To reveal the hidden mysteries of the Bible for the present day,
*   To get Babylon out of the church,
*   The importance of true doctrine,
*   The truth about giving,
*   The incredible story of truth and grace, and
*   Building the strongest church in history.

Dr. Fulcher's uncompromising stance on the consequences of false worship (the importance of true doctrine) has also been particularly prevalent in his teachings. Regarding false doctrine, the man of God has never been a reed shaking in the wind!

Dr. Fulcher has steadfastly preached the gospel to the world via Short-wave Radio and the Internet. There is no doubt that his ministry is the strongest there has been since Jesus walked the earth.

Contents

Chapter One

Impossible

1. Newer members do not fully understand the depth and structure of what made this church as strong as it is, and for the first time in quite a while, someone who was part of this church decided to stop attending.

2. Hebrews 10:25-26 says,

25 Not forsaking the assembling of ourselves together, as the manner of some is; but exhorting one another: and so much the more, as ye see the day approaching.

26 For if we sin wilfully after that we have received the knowledge of the truth, there remaineth no more sacrifice for sins,

3. We believe and practice the commandment given in Hebrews 10:25-26. To my knowledge, we are the only church worldwide that enforces this verse; Hebrews 10:25-26 is the basis for the cornerstone of Jesus Christ's message and the church's establishment.

4. Before I became an adult, I attended my dad's church; he allowed people to attend or miss whenever they wanted. Their reasons were not important. My dad, the pastor, would tell visiting evangelists that the building would be full if everyone in his church attended on the same night; he had a Saturday night crowd and a Sunday night crowd.

5. I grew up in that garbage, and I have never seen a church that can get the entire congregation to attend

consistently. For me, it is a very simple matter because Hebrews 10:25-26 said not to forsake the assembling of ourselves together.

Making a Stand

6. They believe that missing a service does not mean they have forsaken it, but staying out of church for any reason other than one beyond their control means that they have forsaken assembling, at least for that time.

7. This subject caused more people to leave our church than are attending now; since 1978, I have continued my stand in obeying Hebrews 10:25-26. Grace covers the inherent sins of the flesh, but grace will not cover missing a church service.

8. Grace operates on faith, which comes from hearing God's word, and you cannot hear without a preacher, so if you do not attend the church where the preacher is teaching faith, you do not have grace for anything, proving this subject is essential to our salvation.

9. During my ministry, thousands declared that I was a great man of God. Hundreds confessed to seeing angels walking around me. Thousands confessed that my ministry healed them and testified of financial miracles. Some called me something near Jesus in the flesh, while others called me Beelzebub, yet they are no longer with us.

10. Thousands have attended my ministry, yet my current congregation size is tiny compared to most churches. I could have sold out and compromised my stand on Hebrews 10:25-26 at any moment during my

ministry. Had I sold out, I would now have at least twice as many people in my congregation, but depending on the night, I know half of them would choose not to attend because they would come whenever they pleased.

11. I do not believe that is Christianity. Attending church at the appointed time has nothing to do with your job situation, visitors that may show up, or your tiredness. Jesus did not forsake going to the cross even though he was up for twenty-four hours with no sleep. He did not forsake declaring the truth because his mother was late getting to church. Serving God has nothing to do with your choices, feelings, or thoughts. Jesus did not even allow a young man to attend his dad's funeral.

12. Matthew 8:21-22 says,

21 And another of his disciples said unto him, Lord, suffer me first to go and bury my father.

22 But Jesus said unto him, Follow me; and let the dead bury their dead.

13. These principles of Christianity prove that most churches have nothing to do with it. Their only concern is enlarging their congregation, no matter who walks in. Even though I preach a very enlightening message, some still leave because they are unbelievers. They pretend to believe when it is convenient for them. They may go to church to get a new boyfriend or girlfriend, a house, or to feel good about themselves.

3

14. Few genuinely believe there is a God, but if you do, you believe in him no matter what happens in your life. Whether it is good or bad, you believe in God. I teach a message called *The Resurrection*. In it, I say that if you believe in God, you will do something about it. Only an unintelligent person would do nothing.

15. When tough times hit, God wants his followers to run their lives in one direction, but unbelievers will run differently. Since they choose to run their own lives, it proves they are their god because their will reigns superior.

Here for Your Good
16. Romans 13:4 says,

4 For he is the minister of God to thee for good. But if thou do that which is evil, be afraid; for he beareth not the sword in vain: for he is the minister of God, a revenger to execute wrath upon him that doeth evil.

17. The man of God is here for your good, so if he tells you to change your job, there is a reason for it, even though you may like your job. You may make good money while not having to show up on time, but that does not mean the job is good.

18. A job in God's will, flowing in his veins for your life, is good. It does not matter what the job pays, but some who have left this ministry were lazy and did not want to work a regular job; I told some to get away from their lifestyle and leave their current job, which was downtown. I even implemented a plan to help

them while they looked for other employment, but they did not even try.

19. God blesses the fruit of your labor, but you must have a job for that to happen. If your lifestyle gives you full reign of your life and you prey on people, the predator remains unharmed, the prey is injured, and it will destroy your life unless you are strong. A strong person accepts the will of God when he says it is time for a change in your life.

20. I am not saying specific jobs are sinful, but as an allegory, if you stand next to something that emits nuclear radiation, you may not see a change in your cell structure, but changes are occurring. I teach that when you participate in this ministry, you do not have to change your life, but do not be shocked if your life changes.

21. Those who have grown up in my ministry do not understand that this message has delivered them from harmful things. One of my daughters died because she wanted to run her own life. Recently, another daughter chose to go her own way.

22. Some who left have at least called or sent a letter telling me they no longer want to participate in my ministry. Even though they are damned, at least they left appropriately, but when staff members leave and do not let me know, they did not do their job that day. More importantly, they chose the direction they wanted for their life.

23. Being in the message for a long time does not mean you are secure. Serving, worshiping, and following

God is a serious matter. Going to church is the most severe issue in your life. There is nothing more important in your life than serving God.

A Unique Church

24. 1 Corinthians 15:19 says,

19 If in this life only we have hope in Christ, we are of all men most miserable.

25. And Psalms 90:10 says,

10 The days of our years are threescore years and ten; and if by reason of strength they be fourscore years, yet is their strength labour and sorrow; for it is soon cut off, and we fly away.

26. After our seventy years of life are over, what do we have? Nothing in this life is more essential than what you do with Christ. What you decide to do about Jesus will decide your eternal destiny. Those who do not follow Christ will stand before God at the White Throne Judgment to explain why they did not keep his word. No excuse will get them into heaven. In fact, according to the scriptures, which refer to the White Throne Judgment, no one will make it.

27. This church is different and unique; I guarantee that if you do not like how I run this church, you can find one somewhere that will run things the way you like. Many preachers are ready to recruit you, wanting your body in a seat, hoping you will put money in the offering pan; they will let you believe and do what you

6

want. Even if they preach against something you are doing, they will not do anything about it.

28. I do not run my church that way. We will do it the Bible way, which I, as the man of God, have figured out based on the Bible. If not, I will shut the church down and sell it. I do not know or want to do it any other way. I am not looking for an easy way out or a church I can be happy in but then split hell in the middle when I die. I want to attend a church that will get me out of here alive.

29. Many disagree with some things I teach, but I do not understand how anyone can disagree with me on this subject. Hebrews 10:25-26 says it plainly. In fact, in every translation of the Bible, Hebrews 10:25-26 says the same thing.

30. Their way out is to say, "The fact I did not attend a church service that day does not mean I have forsaken God." If you forsake the obedience of the word, which is God, then you have forsaken God, so serving and worshipping God is essential in all our lives.

31. The person who recently left had been in this ministry since birth. They heard the Resurrection message every time I preached it. Their presence and agreement, when they nodded their head, prove they believed it. I have always ended the Resurrection message by saying that if you are intelligent and believe Jesus got out of the ground, you must believe everything else he said.

32. Matthew 12:30 says,

30 He that is not with me is against me; and he that gathereth not with me scattereth abroad.

33. And Matthew 6:33 says,

33 But seek ye first the kingdom of God, and his righteousness; and all these things shall be added unto you.

34. If Jesus raised himself out of the ground, he could put us in the Lake of Fire for not keeping these scriptures. As I read these verses, I wondered how a person could listen for twenty-five years and not taste the word of God in some form. How could they not hear, feel, or see something?

35. Luke 9:62 says,

62 And Jesus said unto him, No man, having put his hand to the plough, and looking back, is fit for the kingdom of God.

36. Some newer church members saw some events occur in recent months where I put people out and allowed them back if they did things correctly, but if someone leaves the church on their own accord, I cannot allow them to return. If you plan to pray for them, you waste your time because this matter is entirely different.

Note That Man
37. 2 Thessalonians 3:14-15 says,

14 And if any man obey not our word by this epistle, note that man, and have no company with him, that he may be ashamed.

15 Yet count him not as an enemy, but admonish him as a brother.

38. When the man of God puts people out of the church, it is for disciplinary reasons. At that point, they are not an enemy. We still consider them brother or sister, but I am disciplining them; I put them out to show that I might allow them back.

39. This person did not leave by choice, but I disciplined them because they walked in error. I put this person out, hoping to shame them, but when you decide to walk away, you have counted the cost alone.

40. Philippians 3:17-19 says,

17 Brethren, be followers together of me, and mark them which walk so as ye have us for an ensample.

18 For many walk, of whom I have told you often, and now tell you even weeping, that they are the enemies of the cross of Christ:

19 Whose end is destruction, whose God is their belly, and whose glory is in their shame, who mind earthly things.

41. And 2 Peter 2:20 says,

20 For if after they have escaped the pollutions of the world through the knowledge of the Lord and Saviour Jesus Christ, they are again entangled therein, and overcome, the latter end is worse with them than the beginning.

42. If you escape this world and its darkness by coming into the light but leave, you return to the things from which God delivered you. I have said many times that a person who has light but rejects it and walks away, their life becomes darker than before they first attended this church.

43. If you talk to someone who has left, you will discover they do not remember anything I taught. I am amazed at how much they forget and how quickly they become traditional again. Their latter end is worse than their beginning because, although they had light, which God took time to give them, they counted it as nothing.

44. Once a person makes a statement, they will fight much harder to support it than if they had not asserted it. Most who have left do not admit they left God; they claim to have left my ministry because they disagreed with me.

45. For them to disagree, the word of God must have convinced them that I was wrong, so they should be able to prove it since they are making such an important decision or disagree by saying that they think or feel a certain way. They are damned because you must have a man of God to do your spiritual thinking, which applies to the Word.

46. 2 Pet 2:21-22 says,

21 For it had been better for them not to have known the way of righteousness, than, after they have known it, to turn from the holy commandment delivered unto them.

22 But it is happened unto them according to the true proverb, The dog is turned to his own vomit again; and the sow that was washed to her wallowing in the mire.

47. These people had the holy word delivered but chose to leave it. Their reasons do not matter because they became more important than the word of God at that point. They will have difficulty finding scripture to prove that I cannot tell them to change their job.

48. Hebrews 13:17 says,

17 Obey them that have the rule over you, and submit yourselves: for they watch for your souls, as they that must give account, that they may do it with joy, and not with grief: for that is unprofitable for you.

49. They had to leave for whatever reason; they disagreed with what I taught or what the word says.

50. 2 Peter 2:22 says,

22 But it is happened unto them according to the true proverb, The dog is turned to his own vomit again; and the sow that was washed to her wallowing in the mire.

51. It is better not to know a single word about God than to know, hear, and be a part of his word but then turn from it.

52. 1 Corinthians 11:27-29 says,

27 Wherefore whosoever shall eat this bread, and drink this cup of the Lord, unworthily, shall be guilty of the body and blood of the Lord.

28 But let a man examine himself, and so let him eat of that bread, and drink of that cup.

29 For he that eateth and drinketh unworthily, eateth and drinketh damnation to himself, <u>not discerning the Lord's body</u>.

53. You must discern the Lord's body, which is the word. As Christians, we deal with the unseen world. We live and move in that which we cannot see.

54. 2 Corinthians 4:16-18 says,

16 For which cause we faint not; but though our outward man perish, yet the inward man is renewed day by day.

17 For our light affliction, which is but for a moment, worketh for us a far more exceeding and eternal weight of glory;

18 While we look not at the things which are seen, but at the things which are not seen: for the things which are seen are temporal; but the things which are not seen are eternal.

55. We do not live by our situation or how we think our life should be.

56. Hebrews 11:1 says,

1 Now faith is the substance of things hoped for, the evidence of things not seen.

57. And Hebrews 11:7 says,

7 By faith Noah, being warned of God of things not seen as yet, moved with fear, prepared an ark to the saving of his house; by the which he condemned the world, and became heir of the righteousness which is by faith.

58. Noah served God by having faith in what he had not yet seen. It had not rained at this point in history.

59. Again, 2 Thessalonians 3:14-16 says,

14 And if any man obey not our word by this epistle, note that man, and have no company with him, that he may be ashamed.

15 Yet count him not as an enemy, but admonish him as a brother.

16 Now the Lord of peace himself give you peace always by all means. The Lord be with you all.

60. 2 Thessalonians 3:14-16 refers to those whom Paul disciplined. When I put people out of the church, we are not to fellowship with them. We should pray for them but not allow them into our homes. We do this with the hope that those I put out will see the error of their ways and come back. If not, they are just like a dog that returns to its vomit and a sow to the mire; it will be worse when they leave than before they heard the word of God.

61. Ephesians 5:11 says,

11 And have no fellowship with the unfruitful works of darkness, but rather reprove them.

62. And 2 Corinthians 6:14 says,

14 Be ye not unequally yoked together with unbelievers: for what fellowship hath righteousness with unrighteousness? and what communion hath light with darkness?

63. If someone who has left this message says hello on the street, you can be nice and say hello back to him or her, but you must not seek fellowship with them.

64. Amos 3:3 says,

3 Can two walk together, except they be agreed?

65. Once a person walks out of the message of Jesus Christ, they are damned, and there is no hope of redemption.

It Is a Race
66. 1 Corinthians 9:24 says,

24 Know ye not that they which run in a race run all, but one receiveth the prize? So run, that ye may obtain.

67. And Hebrews 12:1 says,

1 Wherefore seeing we also are compassed about with so great a cloud of witnesses, let us lay aside every weight, and the sin which doth so easily beset us, and let us run with patience the race that is set before us,

68. We are in a race. We should run and not back up. There is no time to stop running because you have problems. We are in a race, a fight, and a war; we must discern the Lord's body and strive to understand the word.

69. I recently heard a minister on television teaching communion. He said that when you take the wafer, it is not just a wafer; it is the body of Jesus. That is wrong! The Bible is the body of Christ. God did not transform his word into a wafer; he transformed it into flesh and blood and dwelt among us.

70. Many left this ministry saying they did not have to obey Hebrews 10:25-26, but we must discern that the Bible is the Lord's body. When we read the Bible, we are reading about God's nature. When I teach you the truth of God's word, I teach you God's thoughts.

71. Therefore, you should respect that God gave you the truth of his word. God will not save you if you turn aside and no longer walk with it; once you walk away from the truth, your latter end will be worse.

Entangled

72. Again, 2 Peter 2:20-22 says,

20 For if after they have escaped the pollutions of the world through the knowledge of the Lord and Saviour Jesus Christ, they are again entangled therein, and overcome, the latter end is worse with them than the beginning.

21 For it had been better for them not to have known the way of righteousness, than, after they have known it, to turn from the holy commandment delivered unto them.

22 But it is happened unto them according to the true proverb, The dog is turned to his own vomit again; and the sow that was washed to her wallowing in the mire.

73. Everyone is blind and lost before they come to the truth. If they partake of the truth and walk away, they will be even more lost than before coming to the truth. They will be more blind, stupid, and damned than they were before. Every person, who has left this ministry, is damned. I have never changed my position on this subject. If I did not believe I teach the truth of God's word, then there would be room to wiggle.

74. However, I am teaching and applying the truth of God's word. His word gives us great liberty, so you should adamantly and thankfully do the things that give you faith, even if it screws up your plans for Friday night. If it screws up your career opportunity, you should thank God with joy and say that the trade-off is worth it. What you are getting compared to what you are giving up is nothing. Those participating in this ministry have learned and seen many things about God. God's word enlightened them.

75. Strong's definition of the word "enlightened" is [1]

5461 photizo fo-tid'-zo;

- *from 5457; to shed rays, i.e. to shine or transitively to brighten up literally or figuratively:*

76. And Thayer's definition of the word "enlightened" is [2]

5461 photizo-

- *to give light, to shine*
- *to enlighten, to light up, to illumine*
- *to bring to light, to render evident; to cause something to exist and thus come to light and to become clear to all*
- *to enlighten, spiritually, to imbue with saving knowledge*
  - *to instruct, to inform, to teach*
  - *to give understanding to*

77. For most, the Bible was a dead book before they came to this ministry. Some may have had bits and pieces of light from it, but the Bible became illuminated after participating in this ministry of truth. It does this as a fluorescent light illuminates every corner of a room. If the message has illuminated you enough to have one taste of rightly understanding God's word, but then you turn and walk away from it, he said it was impossible for him to renew you.

Two Impossible Things

78. Hebrews 6:18 says that God cannot do two things:

18 That by two immutable things, in which it was impossible for God to lie, we might have a strong consolation, who have fled for refuge to lay hold upon the hope set before us:

79. The first thing God cannot do is lie to the believer, but he employs others to lie to the heathen.

80. 1 Kings 22:20-22 says,

20 And the LORD said, Who shall persuade Ahab, that he may go up and fall at Ramoth-gilead? And one said on this manner, and another said on that manner.

21 And there came forth a spirit, and stood before the LORD, and said, I will persuade him.

22 And the LORD said unto him, Wherewith? And he said, I will go forth, and I will be a lying spirit in the mouth of all his prophets. And he said, Thou shalt persuade him, and prevail also: go forth, and do so.

81. God made the lying spirit so he could say he does not lie; many preachers will teach about that one point by saying that God would heal them and said he could not lie, but they will not talk about the other thing God cannot do because they are afraid.

82. Matthew 12:31 says,

31 Wherefore I say unto you, All manner of sin and blasphemy shall be forgiven unto men: but the blasphemy against the Holy Ghost shall not be forgiven unto men.

83. When God's spirit mixes with Jesus, the word inside a true believer, it creates light or illumination, the Holy Ghost. It is not a feeling you get; it is the illumination of the word.

84. Hebrews 6:4-6 says,

4 For it is impossible for those who were once enlightened, and have tasted of the heavenly gift, and were made partakers of the Holy Ghost,

5 And have tasted the good word of God, and the powers of the world to come,

6 If they shall fall away, to renew them again unto repentance; seeing they crucify to themselves the Son of God afresh, and put him to an open shame.

85. It is the second thing that it is impossible for God to do. If the message of truth has truly illuminated someone and then that person walks away from it, it will be impossible for God to save, redeem, or restore him or her.

86. Some disagree with me by saying that God is merciful, but Hebrews 6:4-6 still says what it says. God said that even he could not renew someone who walks away after receiving the precious word.

87. During my entire ministry, I have only allowed one person to return after she left by her own choice; shortly after returning, she left again and ended up damned. There was another time when a few babes in Christ left by their own choice. They came from another state and were unprepared for what lay in store. The shock destroyed them, and they staggered outside the message, but I allowed them to return through the Bible process; they were an exception because they were still young in the Lord.

88. Walking away from the truth is very dangerous because God said he would not save anyone who has tasted the truth of his word and then leaves. When people walk away, I cannot pray for or restore them, and the body of Christ cannot speak with them either.

89. After someone walks away from God's word, he will not renew them. If I did not believe this, I would not teach it. I know the message I teach illuminates my congregation because some are from various parts of the world, and it has changed their lives. They walk in new footsteps because I teach God's word without opinion or tradition and let the word interpret itself.

90. 1 Corinthians 2:13 says,

13 Which things also we speak, not in the words which man's wisdom teacheth, but which the Holy Ghost teacheth; comparing spiritual things with spiritual.

91. Mary, the mother of Jesus, was the only person who may have genuinely known that the child she carried within her was the word of God. Likewise, I

may be the only person who knows that this message came from God because I am not smart enough to think it all up on my own.

92. Some regard me as thoughtful and intelligent, but they credit me for what God did. I am not more intelligent than anyone else. God has chosen to speak through me; I am merely a vessel. I cannot apologize for having the ability to prove the word of God while others cannot. I am only the spokesman.

93. I am neither smart nor stupid, but the sheep credit me for being smart because of what God does through me. God made his choice. If I thought this message up alone, there would be significant contradictions, but there are no contradictions within the message I teach. I have taught this message since 1970.

94. Each message I teach links into another one, making it a continual message from the first day I started. You will never convince me that a person who sits for one service in this church will not have illumination, so if you claim that you did not understand anything I taught after you have been here for more than five years, you are fighting a losing battle.

95. Isaiah 35:8 says,

8 And an highway shall be there, and a way, and it shall be called The way of holiness; the unclean shall not pass over it; but it shall be for those: the wayfaring men, though fools, shall not err therein.

96. Even if you claim to be a fool, hoping to get out of it, Isaiah 35:8 condemns you; you must be lower than a fool to claim that while you attended this church, you did not understand what I taught.

97. Hebrews 6:1-2 says,

1 Therefore leaving the principles of the doctrine of Christ, let us go on unto perfection; not laying again the foundation of repentance from dead works, and of faith toward God,

2 Of the doctrine of baptisms, and of laying on of hands, and of resurrection of the dead, and of eternal judgment.

98. There are certain things I should not have to teach every week. For example, I teach the truth about Baptism, the Laying on of Hands, and the Resurrection at least once a year. The White Throne Judgment message is another one I regularly teach that should shock sincere people.

99. If you play games, it will not matter to you because you think that God does not mean what he said. You will either be behind the White Throne, judging the damned, or in front of the White Throne, where God will judge you. There, you will try to explain to God why going to work was more important than obeying Hebrews 10:25-26.

100. You cannot claim that grace covers you for missing church because you must attend church to get grace. Grace comes by faith. If you walk away from

this message, you are damned; God cannot and will not save you.

101.   After being in my ministry, you will not tolerate another because they play too many games. They do not understand or teach the truth of God's word; instead, they preach lies. If you agree their preaching is terrible, you have understood or tasted something I taught. If you listen to a true man of God, even briefly, you will understand some of the Bible.

102.   A woman in my congregation managed to get a few hairs from my head for her healing, so it is clear that she got something from my teaching. The most dangerous thing you can do in this life is to participate in this ministry without meaning it.

103.   At first, you may do it ignorantly, but after you listen more than once, you better mean it. God is watching, the Holy Ghost is listening, and Satan is accusing.   Once you confess that you learned something from my teaching, you admit it has illuminated you.   You may not receive all understanding, but you have at least received a taste.

104.   Again, Hebrews 6:4 says,

4 For it is impossible for those who were once enlightened, and have tasted of the heavenly gift, and were made partakers of the Holy Ghost,

Your Latter End
105.   Since the Bible says that your latter end will be worse than your beginning, I will not be surprised

when a judgment or a curse falls on those who leave. I would not even ride down the road in a car with them because I do not know when judgment will strike. I would stay away because I could also feel the curse's effects.

106.   I proved my stance on this matter. A family member died. While she was dying, God told me not to pray for her because she left this message. Some accused me of being mean, hard, and not having any love, but they can go to hell as far as I am concerned. God told me to step aside, and I obeyed. My family member was in this message for years, and then she walked away. The word says that once you have tasted God's word and walk away, your latter end will be worse.

107.   What could be worse? God will judge those who leave and might make their lives a living hell. For example, a young man from West Virginia was part of this ministry during the 1970s. When he left, he did not get mad at me or turn against the doctrine of Christ; he did not want to attend any longer.

108.   Before he left, I looked him in the eyes and told him his life would be a living hell if he walked away from this message. Later, he told his mother that I was right. After he left, his life was a living hell, and he is currently in prison. No one should base their decision on staying because of the story. I am simply showing you the possibilities.

109.   Nevertheless, the worst thing that could happen if you leave is nothing. God may not put you under judgment or bother you until the White Throne

Judgment, so if you leave, the best thing is for judgment to fall upon you at once because at least you know what is happening. However, if you go on your merry way through life, and everything works out great for you, you will believe you were right to leave, but when you stand at the White Throne Judgment, it will be too late.

110.   Again, Hebrews 6:4 says,

4 For it is impossible for those who were once enlightened, and have tasted of the heavenly gift, and were made partakers of the Holy Ghost,

111.   Again, Strong's definition of the word "enlightened" is [3]

5461 photizo fo-tid'-zo;

- *from 5457; to shed rays, i.e. to shine or transitively to brighten up literally or figuratively:*

112.   And Thayer's definition of the word "enlightened" is [4]

5461 photizo-

- *to give light, to shine*
- *to enlighten, to light up, to illumine*
- *to bring to light, to render evident; to cause something to exist and thus come to light and to become clear to all*

25

- *to enlighten, spiritually, to imbue with saving knowledge*
  - *to instruct, to inform, to teach*
  - *to give understanding to*

113.   The English word for *photizo* is photo. When you take a photo, the flash illuminates the dark. It is terrible for people to attend this church, take part, clap their hands, and confess that I am right, but then walk away.

114.   You can walk away as friendly or as an enemy. If you walk away friendly, we will not bother you, but we will be enemies if you walk away as an enemy. Either way, you are damned. The only people I may allow back are those I put out. If I allowed those who left voluntarily to return, this building would be full, but it has nothing to do with me allowing them back.

115.   Once a person leaves, it is out of my hands because the Bible says that it is impossible for God to renew him or her. Some may have left by their own choice, claiming this message did not enlighten them. God made a list.

116.   Again, Hebrews 6:4-6 says,

4 For it is impossible for those who were once enlightened, and have tasted of the heavenly gift, and were made partakers of the Holy Ghost,

5 And have tasted the good word of God, and the powers of the world to come,

6 If they shall fall away, to renew them again unto repentance; seeing they crucify to themselves the Son of God afresh, and put him to an open shame.

117.   Something on this list will apply. For example, *"partakers of the Holy Ghost"* means those given an understanding of the word. Jesus was nailed to a cross and murdered. His death was torturous, bleeding with nails in his hands and feet, so as it says in Hebrews 6:4-6: if you tasted God's word; if God gave you understanding, but you still walk away, you just did that to him again. At that point, you are not worthy.

118.   Philippians 3:18 says,

18 For many walk, of whom I have told you often, and now tell you even weeping, that they are the enemies of the cross of Christ:

119.   By crucifying him afresh, you hold him to open shame again and become his enemy.

120.   Again, Hebrews 6:6 says,

6 If they shall fall away, to renew them again unto repentance; seeing they crucify to themselves the Son of God afresh, and put him to an open shame.

121.   God is big and powerful and knows about everything. He made universes and worlds, threw Satan out of heaven, and later threw the fallen Sons of God out and bound them into judgment. He created complicated human beings; we cannot even come close to making anything like ourselves.

122.   The same powerful deity said that if you have the truth, tasted, seen, or felt it, but then you walk away, even he could not renew you. Think about the thousands who have walked away from this message and have damned themselves for doing it.

123.   I am putting pressure on my congregation to do what the word says to do. You will not come to my ministry and float out on a flowery bed of ease. I pressure you to get us out of here alive and perfected so we will have eternal life. I want you to obey the word of God because I want to please God, and if I do not please him, even he cannot save me, so I will continue to pressure my congregation until the message perfects them.

124.   Hebrews 6:4-6 of the New International Version says,

4 It is impossible for those who have once been enlightened, who have tasted the heavenly gift, who have shared in the Holy Spirit,

5 who have tasted the goodness of the word of God and the powers of the coming age,

6 if they fall away, to be brought back to repentance, because to their loss they are crucifying the Son of God all over again and subjecting him to public disgrace.

125.   And Hebrews 6:4-6 of the New King James Version says,

4 For it is impossible for those who were once enlightened, and have tasted the heavenly gift, and have become partakers of the Holy Spirit,

5 and have tasted the good word of God and the powers of the age to come,

6 if they fall away, to renew them again to repentance, since they crucify again for themselves the Son of God, and put Him to an open shame.

126. *"To fall away"* means that you may still believe in it but are not doing it.

127. Hebrews 6:4-6 of the New American Standard Version says,

4 For in the case of those who have once been enlightened and have tasted of the heavenly gift and have been made partakers of the Holy Spirit,

5 and have tasted the good word of God and the powers of the age to come,

6 and then have fallen away, it is impossible to renew them again to repentance, since they again crucify to themselves the Son of God, and put Him to open shame.

128. And Hebrews 6:4-6 of the Living Bible says,

4 There is no use trying to bring you back to the Lord again if you have once understood the Good News and tasted for yourself the good things of heaven and shared in the Holy Spirit,

29

5 and know how good the Word of God is, and felt the mighty powers of the world to come,

6 and then have turned against God. You cannot bring yourself to repent again if you have nailed the Son of God to the cross again by rejecting him, holding him up to mocking and to public shame.

Turning Against God

129.　　Genesis 3:8 says,

8 And they heard the voice of the Lord God walking in the garden in the cool of the day: and Adam and his wife hid themselves from the presence of the Lord God amongst the trees of the garden.

130.　　This day was an exciting and climatic time for the voice of the Lord; the voice often communicated with Adam because they had a meeting place. The voice of the Lord showed up at the appointed meeting place.

131.　　When he arrived, Adam and his woman were not there. They did not attend that night because they had something else to do. They just discovered nakedness. They wanted to hang out with the trees but did not attend church that day.

132.　　Some who have left may say they have not turned against God because they believe they only walked from this church, but turning against God means turning against his word. They are turning against Hebrews 10:25-26 by staying out of the church.

After they walk away, they cannot repent because they have crucified Christ again to an open shame.

133.   Remember, turning against God means turning against the word or not believing in it. If you say you are not against it but do not believe it, you are deluding yourself because it is the same thing. If you believe that there is a God, that there is a word, that he raised himself from the dead, and that he was big enough to throw Satan out of heaven, why would you not want to obey Hebrews 10:25-26?

134.   Again, Hebrews 10:26 says,

26 For if we sin wilfully after that we have received the knowledge of the truth, there remaineth no more sacrifice for sins,

135.   And Hebrews 6:4-6 of the Revised Standard Version says,

4 For it is impossible to restore again to repentance those who have once been enlightened, who have tasted the heavenly gift, and have become partakers of the Holy Spirit,

5 and have tasted the goodness of the word of God and the powers of the age to come,

6 if they then commit apostasy, since they crucify the Son of God on their own account and hold him up to contempt.

136.   If you break and walk from the word, you hold him up to contempt.

137.   1 John 2:4 says,

4 He that saith, I know him, and keepeth not his commandments, is a liar, and the truth is not in him.

138.   And John 14:15 says,

15 If ye love me, keep my commandments.

139.   And John 14:23-24 says,

23 Jesus answered and said unto him, If a man love me, he will keep my words: and my Father will love him, and we will come unto him, and make our abode with him.

24 He that loveth me not keepeth not my sayings: and the word which ye hear is not mine, but the Father's which sent me.

140.   One of his sayings tells us to praise him in the dance. Another saying tells us that God loves cheerful givers. We find another saying in Hebrews 10:25,

25 Not forsaking the assembling of ourselves together, as the manner of some is; but exhorting one another: and so much the more, as ye see the day approaching.

Impossible

141.   And Hebrews 6:4 says,

4 For it is impossible for those who were once enlightened, and have tasted of the heavenly gift, and were made partakers of the Holy Ghost,

142.   Strong's definition of the word "impossible" is [5]

102 adunatos ad-oo'-nat-os;

- from 1 as a negative particle and 1415; unable, i.e. weak literally or figuratively; passively, impossible:

143.   And   Thayer's   definition   of   the   word "impossible" is [6]

102 adunatos-

- without strength, impotent, powerless, weakly, disabled
- unable to be done, impossible

144.   According to Websters's II New Riverside Dictionary, the word "impossible" means [7]

- *Not capable of existing or taking place.*
- *Unlikely to happen or be done.*
- *Unacceptable.*
- *Difficult to tolerate or deal with.*

145.   There is no better word to say we cannot do something than the word impossible; Hebrews 6:4 says that it is impossible, weak, and unable to be done, so God cannot restore people once they have tasted his word and walked away.

146.   Traditional churches do not preach this message because they restore people to keep benches full. If you cannot attend church for reasons beyond your control, then you are not guilty of forsaking God's commandment found in Hebrews 10:25-26.

147.   God said this was impossible even for him. Knowing that even God cannot save some people shocks the world. God cannot save those who have tasted and walked from his word. It does not apply to people learning this message for the first time or those who have been or are currently attending a false church prior to learning this message.   You cannot be enlightened in a false church because a little leaven leavens the whole lump. All you need is a taste. You do not need to have the whole pie.

148.   Again, Hebrews 6:6 says,

6 If they shall fall away, to renew them again unto repentance; seeing they crucify to themselves the Son of God afresh, and put him to an open shame.

149.   Strong's definition of the phrase "they shall fall away" is [8]

3895 parapipto par-ap-ip'-to;

- *from 3844 and 4098; to <u>fall aside</u>, i.e. figuratively to <u>apostatize</u>:*

And Thayer's definition of the phrase "they shall fall away" is [9]

3895 parapipto-

34

- *to fall beside a person or thing*
- *to slip aside*
  - o *to deviate from the right path, to turn aside, to wander*
  - o *to error*
  - o *to fall away from the true faith: from worship of Jehovah Yahweh*

4098 pipto-

- *to descend from a higher place to a lower*
  - o *to fall either from or upon, to be thrust down*
  - o *metaphorically, to fall under judgment, to came under condemnation*
- *to descend from an erect to a prostrate position*
  - o *to fall down*
    - ▪ *to be prostrated, to fall prostrate*
    - ▪ *used of those overcome by terror or astonishment or grief or under the attack of an evil spirit or of falling dead suddenly*
    - ▪ *the dismemberment of a corpse by decay*
    - ▪ *to prostrate oneself*
    - ▪ *used of suppliants and persons rendering homage or worship to one*
    - ▪ *to fall out, to fall from, that is, shall perish or be lost*
    - ▪ *to fall down, to fall into ruin: of buildings, walls, etc.*

- o *to be cast down from a state of prosperity*
  - *to fall from a state of uprightness*
  - *to perish, that is, to come to an end, to disappear, to cease;*
  - *used of virtues*
  - *to lose authority, no longer have force; used of sayings, precepts, etc.*
  - *to be removed from power by death*
  - *to fail to participate in, to miss a share in*

150. God said it is impossible, *incapable, cannot be done*, for him to renew people who have fallen away in apostasy. Those in religious circles have heard of apostasy many times, but some do not know what it means.

151. According to the International Standard Bible Encyclopedia, the word "Apostate" means [10]

a-pos'-ta-si, a-pos'-tat

- *he apostasia, a standing away from: I.e. a falling away, a withdrawal, a defection.*
- *forsaking worship and spiritual living Heb 10:25-31;*
- *unbelief Heb 3:12.*
- *In classical Greek, apostasy signified revolt from a military commander.*

- *An apostate's defection from the faith may be intellectual.*

Two Classes of People

152.   If you walk away from God and the body of Christ, you have defected to Satan's side of the war. Be assured that there are only two classes of people in the world: God's people and the devil's people. You are either on God's side or Satan's side. They may call themselves many different names, but there are only two classes of people.

153.   As the last definition describes, you can still be in a place but leave that place in your mind. Most of the time that is the way it happens. They leave within their minds before they physically leave. They have been around the truth long enough to know it is correct, so they must go through some intellectual process as they talk themselves into leaving. For example, before people get a divorce, they must leave their spouse in their minds and then file for divorce.

154.   To this day, only one person who left by his or her choice has surprised me because I usually know in advance. If I did not know someone planned to leave, I knew he or she was dying spiritually. I am not a miracle worker; God is. If God's word does not stop or change you, then I cannot do anything as a father, man, or person to change you.

155.   Those who listen and follow my ministry know I have no children, wives, girlfriends, or friends regarding God. Like those who follow this ministry,

my earthly family must live by God's word. My example is Jesus Christ.

156.   Luke 8:19-21 says,

19 Then came to him his mother and his brethren, and could not come at him for the press.

20 And it was told him by certain which said, Thy mother and thy brethren stand without, desiring to see thee.

21 And he answered and said unto them, My mother and my brethren are these which hear the word of God, and do it.

157.   In Luke 8:19-21, Jesus did not stop the service to give his mother a seat in the front row. She was late. It is always your earthly family that will push and try you.

158.   Matthew 13:57 says,

57 And they were offended in him. But Jesus said unto them, A prophet is not without honour, save in his own country, and in his own house.

Defecting

159.   The man of God's earthly family always gives him the least respect because they cannot see past the veil of flesh. I love my earthly family, but I do not love them more than I love God's word. If my congregation must measure up to God's word, my earthly family members must, too.

160.   If people in the congregation walk away, they are damned. Likewise, if a person from my earthly family walks away, he or she is damned as well. You cannot make it because you are related to me by blood. You will only get in if you are related to me by faith. Faith is the evidence that you are related to me. My family is those who follow this message.

161.   I must draw the line and say this is the way it is. If we do not stand for something, we will fall for anything. Most churches compete, trying to enlarge their crowd. I am not competing with anyone. I am trying to perfect those who want me to perfect them. If only two people are left, I will teach them the truth of God's word.

162.   If no one wants to hear my message, I will sit alone and keep my understanding of the truth for myself. I will not compromise God's word, regardless of what people think of me. Other ministers cannot teach this message because half their church would leave, or the minister would have to put them out. Doing so would cut their salaries in half, so teaching this message is impossible for them; they are *unable* to teach it. Remember that the word apostasy means to defect. I will not defect.

163.   Again, Hebrews 6:6 says,

6 If they shall fall away, to renew them again unto repentance; seeing they crucify to themselves the Son of God afresh, and put him to an open shame.

164.   Strong's definition of the word "renew" is [11]

340 anakainizo an-ak-ahee-nid'-zo;

- *from 303 and a derivative of 2537; to restore:*

165.   And Thayer's definition of the word "renew" is
[12]

340 anakainizo-

- *to renew, renovate*

166.   If they fall away, it is impossible for God to restore them because they ***"crucify to themselves the Son of God afresh, and put him to an open shame."***

167.   Hebrews 6:6 of the New International Version says,

6 if they fall away, to be brought back to repentance, because to their loss they are crucifying the Son of God all over again and subjecting him to public disgrace.

168.   And Hebrews 6:6 of the Revised Standard Version says,

6 if they then commit apostasy, since they crucify the Son of God on their own account and hold him up to contempt.

169.   And Hebrews 6:6 of the Living Bible says,

6 and then have turned against God. You cannot bring yourself to repent again if you have nailed the Son of God to the cross again by rejecting him, holding him up to mocking and to public shame.

170.   Each version of the Bible agrees. When you reject Jesus Christ, you nail him to the cross again. When you reject the word, you reject him because John 1:14 says,

14 And the Word was made flesh, and dwelt among us, and we beheld his glory, the glory as of the only begotten of the Father, full of grace and truth.

171.   Strong's definition of the phrase "crucify afresh" is [13]

388 anastauroo an-as-tow-ro'-o;

- *from 303 and 4717; to recrucify figuratively:*

4717 stauroo stow-ro'-o;

- *from 4716; to impale on the cross; figuratively, to extinguish subdue passion or selfishness:*

4716 stauros stow-ros';

- *from the base of 2476; a stake or post as set upright, i.e. specifically a pole or cross as an instrument of capital punishment; figuratively, exposure to death, i.e. self-denial; by implication, the atonement of Christ:*

172.   And Thayer's definition of the phrase "crucify afresh" is [14]

388 anastauroo-

- *to raise up upon a cross, crucify*

4717 stauroo-

- *to stake, to drive down stakes*
- *to fortify with driven stakes, to palisade*
- *to crucify:*
- *to crucify one*
- *metaphorically, to crucify the flesh, destroy its power utterly the nature of the figure implying that the destruction is attended with intense pain*

173.   When you impale something, you put it there or drive it in. You thrust Jesus back on the cross if you reject today's message. Even though Jesus Christ died, bled for you, and gave the word so you could be like him, you are saying to hell with him.

174.   You stick him back on the cross and impale him. You do not appreciate what he did for you, where he brought you from, and the life he planned for you. You must know that if God is on your side, your life must be better than if he is not.

175.   Again, Hebrews 6:6 says,

6 If they shall fall away, to renew them again unto repentance; seeing they crucify to themselves the Son of God afresh, and put him to an open shame.

176.   Strong's definition of the phrase "and put him to an open shame" is [15]

3856   paradeigmatizo par-ad-igue-mat-id'-zo;

- *from 3844 and 1165; to show alongside the public, i.e. expose to infamy:*

1165   deigmatizo digh-mat-id'-zo;

- *from 1164; to exhibit:*

1164   deigma digh'-mah;

- *from the base of 1166; a specimen as shown:*

177.   And Thayer's definition of the phrase "and put him to an open shame" is [16]

3856   paradeigmatizo-

- *to set forth as a public example, to make an example of; in a bad sense:*
- *to hold up to infamy*
- ***to expose to public disgrace***

1166   deiknuo-

- ***to show, expose to the eyes***
- *metaphorically,*
  - *to give evidence or proof of a thing*
  - *to show by words or to teach*

Fellowship

178.   Whoever forsakes God's word impales him to the cross.   They intend to *exhibit* him, showing everyone that he is useless to them.   They would stay

43

and obey his word if they believed he was useful. If they believe he resurrected, they will keep his word. Despite knowing this, some still fellowship with people who walk away.

179.   Ephesians 5:11 says,

11 And have no fellowship with the unfruitful works of darkness, but rather reprove them.

180.   And 2 Corinthians 6:17 says,

17 Wherefore come out from among them, and be ye separate, saith the Lord, and touch not the unclean thing; and I will receive you,

181.   And 2 Timothy 3:5 says,

5 Having a form of godliness, but denying the power thereof: from such turn away.

182.   And Amos 3:3 says,

3 Can two walk together, except they be agreed?

183.   And 2 Corinthians 6:14 says,

14 Be ye not unequally yoked together with unbelievers: for what fellowship hath righteousness with unrighteousness? and what communion hath light with darkness?

184.   Why would anyone fellowship people who impaled, exposed, and *exhibited* Jesus Christ, just as they did the first time they crucified him? Especially

when we have more to lose now. In Jesus' day, it was literal. Today, he illuminates us.

185. Anyone who denies Christ and walks away from him has spit on Christ, just like they did in the Bible. You slap and turn on him. You make a spectacle out of him and make him powerless in your life. You dethrone him and make him nothing because you had the chance to walk in truth, but you chose to walk away.

186. *"To show and expose to the eyes"* means showing that you have walked away from God. When you walk from God, all the others who walked from God pat you on the back and say you made the right choice. An old proverb says, *"Birds of a feather flock together;"* those in a sinking boat want to take as many with them as possible to feel good about themselves.

Anathema Maranatha

187. Again, Hebrews 6:4-5 says,

4 For it is impossible for those who were once enlightened, and have tasted of the heavenly gift, and were made partakers of the Holy Ghost,

5 And have tasted the good word of God, and the powers of the world to come,

188. If you walk away, these five things make you Anathema Maranatha.

189. 1 Corinthians 16:22 says,

22 If any man love not the Lord Jesus Christ, let him be Anathema Maranatha.

190.   Strong's definition of the word "Anathema" is
[17]

331 anathema an-ath'-em-ah;

- *from 394; a religious ban or concretely excommunicated thing or person:*

191.   And   Strong's   definition   of   the   word
"Maranatha" is [18]

3134 maran atha mar'-an ath'-ah;

- *of Aramaic origin meaning our Lord has come; maranatha, i.e. an exclamation of the approaching divine judgment:*

192.   One of the five things listed in Hebrews 6:4-5 says that if you were once enlightened, the message has even enlightened the children in this church.

193.   Isaiah 35:8 says,

8 And an highway shall be there, and a way, and it shall be called The way of holiness; the unclean shall not pass over it; but it shall be for those: the wayfaring men, though fools, shall not err therein.

194.   If there are fools in my congregation, I have enlightened them. The next item on the list of the five things is *"to taste the heavenly gift."* There may be some who have not tasted the heavenly gift. They may

have only smelled or heard it, but the heavenly gift is eternal life, which means you caught a glimpse of eternity and want to be part of it more than this life.

195.   Everyone is a partaker of the Holy Ghost, including the children, so if they attend this church, feel the spirit of God, and hear the word of God, it illuminates them; they are partakers of the Holy Ghost.

196.   *"Tasting the good word of God"* means that if it changed or enhanced your life, you understood it, enjoyed it, and received it.

197.   *"The powers of the world to come"* means you believe I am training you to rule worlds. You have a glimpse of it through faith and the word of God. It means I revealed to you that this is coming, and you can be a part of it.

198.   If you have any of the last things mentioned and then walk away, you have condemned yourself. Some say they did not turn against God but turned away from my message and me, yet they sat here as a witness that I am preaching the word. To turn against what I preach means those who walked away have turned against the word because they left over a disagreement.

199.   No one who has left my ministry by their choice has ever proved that what I teach is wrong. Some thought they knew more than me and debated, but I refuted them with scripture. God said that it is impossible for God to save you once you walk away; it is something even God cannot do.

200.   2 Peter 2:20 says,

20 For if after they have escaped the pollutions of the world through the knowledge of the Lord and Saviour Jesus Christ, they are again entangled therein, and overcome, the latter end is worse with them than the beginning.

201.   Anyone following this ministry can get mad at me and leave anytime. Some try to justify themselves by disagreeing with me on a particular subject; if they are wrong about the subject in question, they damn themselves forever. However, if they are correct and intelligent, they should be able to prove their point with the Bible, and then I could concede.

202.   It is unlikely God would give a sheep more knowledge than the shepherd. They may see it before me, but I will get there. In most cases, I will be the one to lead them there. Anything short of staying in this message is damnation to those who follow it. Once people walk away, their light becomes dark, and they are worse off than before.

203.   2 Peter 2:21 says,

21 For it had been better for them not to have known the way of righteousness, than, after they have known it, to turn from the holy commandment delivered unto them.

204.   I must walk if I am at one place and want to go to another, but if I stop before I get there, I will not arrive. I still have my goal, but I will not get there. To get there, I must continue walking. I cannot stop. In

comparison, if I stop in God and do not make it all the way, he moves on while I am still. I will never catch up.

205. Similarly, if you walk away, you must justify yourself by taking all the truth you learned, shouted about, and agreed with and attempt to prove it wrong. It starts by picking on the man of God's personality. Some will say I am abusive, mean, do not have any love, and am bullheaded; they will argue that I think I know everything and that I think I am God.

206. They pick on the carrier rather than the message. They try to justify themselves by saying they are right to leave because I have a bad attitude. Even if they agree with my teaching, my bad attitude is their excuse for leaving.

207. However, the Bible says that God cannot save you if you walk away, so if you leave this church and go to another, your only chance is to find another church that teaches the truth of God's word. If the minister is a real man of God, he will preach and enforce the same message. His style or tone might differ, but he will preach the same message.

208. 2 Peter 1:1 says,

1 Simon Peter, a servant and an apostle of Jesus Christ, to them that have obtained like precious faith with us through the righteousness of God and our Saviour Jesus Christ:

209. And 1 Corinthians 1:10 says,

10 Now I beseech you, brethren, by the name of our Lord Jesus Christ, that ye all speak the same thing, and that there be no divisions among you; but that ye be perfectly joined together in the same mind and in the same judgment.

210.　If you move to China to find another church, you will still have to humble yourself to God's word, or you will go to hell in China.　Those who left by choice clapped their hands and said hallelujah while they were here, but before leaving, they left in their mind, where they suddenly discovered things they suspected all along yet said nothing before leaving because they felt it was not the time.　The more such people justify themselves by not liking me or someone in the church, the more they will lose the concept of truth to tradition until they eventually turn to a reprobate mind.

211.　Romans 1:28 says,

28 And even as they did not like to retain God in their knowledge, God gave them over to a reprobate mind, to do those things which are not convenient;

212.　And 2 Timothy 3:2 says,

2 For men shall be lovers of their own selves, covetous, boasters, proud, blasphemers, disobedient to parents, unthankful, unholy,

Why Not Saturday?
213.　Why would people leave God's word if they did not love themselves more than they loved God?

They should speak with others who run their own lives and see how many commit suicide or go shipwreck.

214.   It is better to have God in your boat than not to have him there. I told a person several years ago to measure up or get out. They chose to get out. Before they left, they accused me of not loving my congregation and ruining every Friday night for them because it was one of the two mandatory church services, the other being Sunday afternoon.   They asked why I did not have the mandatory church service on Saturday instead of Friday.

215.   It was when I came up with the philosophy that if I changed it to Saturday, they would protest because that was the big night out. If I changed it to Sunday, they would be too tired. Monday is the beginning of the week, and they do not feel like doing anything. On Tuesday, they are just getting back into their role. On Wednesday, they want to go out and do something.

216.   Which day do I choose?   Moreover, how is hearing God's word ruining your Friday night? What are you doing that is more important? How can you improve your life by doing something else on Friday night? It is only a few hours, so why can't you move your lifestyle around that time? Isn't God worth it?

217.   Jesus died on the cross and gave his whole life for us. Why can't you do that if he wants your Friday and Sunday? Besides, I go out and do something after church on Friday nights; I delay it for the important thing.

218.   The word says not to forsake.   Although I picked Friday night, if I chose another, which would be convenient? They have their life planned and have things to do. They usually sit at home arguing about what they want to do. By 11 p.m., they are mad because they did not decide and blame their spouse.

219.   If you love God, you should want to attend church on Friday and Sunday to fill your tank. You have the other five days of the week. God asks you to attend church for two days, but you should serve him all week.

220.   He gave us so much freedom through grace that we can enjoy ourselves, attend church, bring our Bibles, and learn about God. I would rather have him in my boat than not have him there. I would prefer he bless my children than not have him at all.

221.   2 Timothy 3:2-4 says,

2 For men shall be lovers of their own selves, covetous, boasters, proud, blasphemers, disobedient to parents, unthankful, unholy,

3 Without natural affection, trucebreakers, false accusers, incontinent, fierce, despisers of those that are good,

4 Traitors, heady, highminded, lovers of pleasures more than lovers of God;

222.   If God gives you a chance to hear the truth of his word, but you will not keep it and later walk away, you are a traitor! "Heady" means self-willed and

arrogant; you think you are smart enough to figure it out. Some argue that if they could work on Friday, they could put more into the offering.

223.   1 Samuel 15:22 says,

22 And Samuel said, Hath the LORD as great delight in burnt offerings and sacrifices, as in obeying the voice of the LORD? Behold, to obey is better than sacrifice, and to hearken than the fat of rams.

224.   This church is real. It is not about the offering, although it is essential for you. I want you to please God first and put the offering second; I could tell my congregation that they do not have to attend Friday nights, allowing everyone to go out and get a second job and give more in the offering, but I want my congregation to obey.

225.   A high-minded person thinks they are better than everyone else. Those who are lovers of pleasure are selfish and self-serving; they love themselves more than they love God. They want to please themselves. Their inner man becomes a slave to their flesh's desires, so the Friday night service interferes with its wishes.

226.   They cannot do something on Tuesday night because it is not Friday, so they become lovers of pleasure and find a minister who lets them have Friday nights off to fulfill their desires; they want a preacher who preaches the truth but does not enforce it.

227.   2 Timothy 4:3-4 says,

3 For the time will come when they will not endure sound doctrine; but after their own lusts shall they heap to themselves teachers, having itching ears;

4 And they shall turn away their ears from the truth, and shall be turned unto fables.

228.   And 1 Timothy 4:1 says,

1 Now the Spirit speaketh expressly, that in the latter times some shall depart from the faith, giving heed to seducing spirits, and doctrines of devils;

229.   They want a preacher to tell them what they want to hear. I am not that type of preacher! They want to serve God their way. They will say, "Me and God have our own thing going; we will work it out ourselves." Not if you do not have the word, and the word says that you must have a man of God; the man of God says that you should be in church on Friday and Sunday because I care about you.

From Such Turn Away
230.   2 Timothy 3:5 says,

5 Having a form of godliness, but denying the power thereof: from such turn away.

231.   "Power" is the word, which means they deny the word. The Bible says, *"From such turn away."* It does not mean you continue to love, fellowship, pray, beg them to return, or hope they will return.

232.   If I put someone out, you can pray for him or her and treat the person as a brother or sister, not as an enemy, but if he or she chooses to walk away - *"from such turn away."* You may think I am hard, but God's word says to do it. I am only repeating it. If you want to get mad at someone, get mad at God. He put it in there. Do not get mad at the carrier. If you walk away, you crucify Jesus Christ afresh.

233.   The God I serve, the one who gave me my freedom, is the same one who will give me eternal life. You drive nails into his hands by leaving, impale him on the cross, and hold him up to public shame. At that point, I have no use for you. To me, you have become the lowest piece of crap on earth. I do not care who you are; if you walk away, you no longer exist. Remember, in this scenario, I did not cut you off; you cut yourself off by your actions. In my mind, when you walk away from this message, you no longer exist. You are dead and gone.

234.   2 Timothy 3:6 says,

6 For of this sort are they which creep into houses, and lead captive silly women laden with sins, led away with divers lusts,

235.   I find it amazing that the moment someone leaves, many who walked away years before will try to comfort that person and congratulate him or her for coming out. You may not know that some who have left might want to return.

236.   The Bible says, *"there remaineth no more sacrifice for sins,"* once you put him to an open shame.

55

The fact that they quickly discovered you walked away proves you have put Jesus to an open shame. Some may say they did not turn against God; they just left my ministry, but I say they did turn against God because God is the word.

237.   John 1:1 says,

1 In the beginning was the Word, and the Word was with God, and the Word was God.

238.   And John 1:14 says,

14 And the Word was made flesh, and dwelt among us, and we beheld his glory, the glory as of the only begotten of the Father, full of grace and truth.

239.   And 1 Tim 3:16 says,

16 And without controversy great is the mystery of godliness: God was manifest in the flesh, justified in the Spirit, seen of angels, preached unto the Gentiles, believed on in the world, received up into glory.

240.   The Bible is Jesus' body put into words so we can read and absorb him. When he gets in you, it comes back to life. The Bible is God's body, and we should discern it. That means we must comprehend, know, and see it. The word says not to forsake the assembling of ourselves together. It also says not to walk away.

241.   2 Timothy 3:7-10 says,

7 Ever learning, and never able to come to the knowledge of the truth.

8 Now as Jannes and Jambres withstood Moses, so do these also resist the truth: men of corrupt minds, reprobate concerning the faith.

9 But they shall proceed no further: for their folly shall be manifest unto all men, as theirs also was.

10 But thou hast fully known my doctrine, manner of life, purpose, faith, longsuffering, charity, patience,

242.   Jannes and Jambres did not call Moses a devil or say he was false; they just wanted a part of the pie.

Reprobate
243.   Titus 1:13-16 says,

13 This witness is true. Wherefore rebuke them sharply, that they may be sound in the faith;

14 Not giving heed to Jewish fables, and commandments of men, that turn from the truth.

15 Unto the pure all things are pure: but unto them that are defiled and unbelieving is nothing pure; but even their mind and conscience is defiled.

16 They profess that they know God; but in works they deny him, being abominable, and disobedient, and unto every good work reprobate.

244.   In all church circles, one word puts fear into them: reprobate. The word "reprobate" comes from apostasy, which is what a person does when they walk away from the truth. Once a person walks away from the truth, their mind is no longer sealed and protected by God's word, and he turns them over to a reprobate mind. A reprobate mind is destitute of any truth or light.

245.   Strong's definition of the word "reprobate" is [19]

96 adokimos ad-ok'-ee-mos;

- *from 1 as a negative particle and 1384; unapproved, i.e. rejected; by implication, worthless literally or morally:*

KJV-- castaway, rejected, reprobate.

3988 ma'ac maw-as';

- *a primitive root; to spurn; also intransitively to disappear:*

KJV-- abhor, cast away off, contemn, despise, disdain, become loathe some, melt away, refuse, reject, reprobate, X utterly, vile person.

246.   And Thayer's definition of the word "reprobate" is [20]

96 adokimos-

- *not standing the test, not approved: properly used of metals and coins*
- *that which does not prove itself as it should: unfit for, unproved, spurious, reprobate*

247.   And Brown-Driver-Brigg's definition of the word "reprobate" is [21]

3988 ma'ac-

- *to reject, to despise, to refuse*
  - *Qal*
    - *to reject, to refuse*
    - *to despise*
  - *Niphal to be rejected*
  - *Niphal to flow, to run*

248.   Once a person walks away from God, he gives their mind to Satan, who takes possession. That person ran from God and rejected him, so if you leave the truth, you reject light; you did not stand the test, and God disapproves of you. You become a castaway and worthless.

249.   Matthew 12:31-32 says,

31 Wherefore I say unto you, All manner of sin and blasphemy shall be forgiven unto men: but the blasphemy against the Holy Ghost shall not be forgiven unto men.

32 And whosoever speaketh a word against the Son of man, it shall be forgiven him: but whosoever speaketh against the Holy Ghost, it shall not be forgiven him, neither in this world, neither in the world to come.

250.   The Son of man is Jesus Christ or the word, and the Holy Ghost is the enlightenment of the word.

251.   Luke 11:23 says,

23 He that is not with me is against me: and he that gathereth not with me scattereth.

252.   It means you are either on God's or the devil's side.

253.   1 John 2:18-21 says,

18 Little children, it is the last time: and as ye have heard that antichrist shall come, even now are there many antichrists; whereby we know that it is the last time.

19 They went out from us, but they were not of us; for if they had been of us, they would no doubt have continued with us: but they went out, that they might be made manifest that they were not all of us.

20 But ye have an unction from the Holy One, and ye know all things.

21 I have not written unto you because ye know not the truth, but because ye know it, and that no lie is of the truth.

254.   Why would anyone want to fellowship someone who walked away from the truth? If this person lives with you, be cordial, but do not be buddy-buddy or fellowship with him or her. If you see someone on the street who has left, be nice if he or she

is nice; react to the vapor thereof. You can speak and be nice, but you should not recruit this person or try to find him or her.

255. They cannot manifest what they are in my church because neither the power of God's word nor I will let them, so they cannot be hypocrites and attend my church. Hypocrites must go elsewhere because they are unfruitful works of darkness; light and darkness cannot dwell together. Two cannot walk together, except they be agreed (Amos 3:3). *"From such turn away."*

256. Philippians 3:17-19 says,

17 Brethren, be followers together of me, and mark them which walk so as ye have us for an ensample.

18 For many walk, of whom I have told you often, and now tell you even weeping, that they are the enemies of the cross of Christ:

19 Whose end is destruction, whose God is their belly, and whose glory is in their shame, who mind earthly things.

257. A man died on the cross for us. If you have tasted the heavenly gift and have been in the house of God, but you walk away, you crucify him afresh. You become an enemy of the act that took place on the cross because you are using it to kill him again. That is how serious it is to have truth but walk away from it.

258. Acts 13:46 says,

46 Then Paul and Barnabas waxed bold, and said, It was necessary that the word of God should first have been spoken to you: but seeing ye put it from you, and judge yourselves unworthy of everlasting life, lo, we turn to the Gentiles.

259.   You can become an enemy of the cross and judge yourself unworthy of everlasting life.

260.   Ephesians 5:11-12 says,

11 And have no fellowship with the unfruitful works of darkness, but rather reprove them.

12 For it is a shame even to speak of those things which are done of them in secret.

Not Fit

261.   Luke 9:62 says,

62 And Jesus said unto him, No man, having put his hand to the plough, and looking back, is fit for the kingdom of God.

262.   Anyone who leaves this ministry is not fit to be among the body of Christ, nor are they worthy to enter the kingdom of God. You may think that is very hard, but that is the word of God.

263.   Matthew 12:30 says,

30 He that is not with me is against me; and he that gathereth not with me scattereth abroad.

264.   People who walk away are not worthy of our prayers, fellowship, worry, or concern. No matter how much I care for a person, once they leave, I no longer care for them as I did. I am dead, and Christ is alive. God gives everyone a chance. I cannot make anyone accept the truth; I can only tell you the truth.

265.   When someone walks away from this ministry, I may hurt and suffer in the flesh, but I cannot change it. If you do not want to do it God's way, then there will be a parting of the way at some time. You cannot run your life better than God because he will show you are wrong.

266.   Again, if you ever walk away from this message, the worst thing that can happen to you is nothing, but if God cares and takes notice, terrible things will happen in your life because he wants to teach you something. It does not mean you can return; he wants you to know you messed up.

267.   If I put you out, I am protecting and getting your attention to let you know you are messing up. It is better if the man of God puts you out than it is for you to leave by your choice. Once you choose to leave, God does not give you any more chances, and the body of Christ cannot fellowship you.

268.   Some may say I am trying to control people by telling my congregation not to fellowship with those who walk away. They are wrong. I am only telling you what the Bible says on this subject. God will not save you if you do what you want; you must do what the Bible says.

269.   We should act decent toward those who leave by their own choice. For example, I recently talked to someone who left because he approached me and shook my hand. I returned his handshake because he had correctly left the church and did not leave as an enemy. He did not want to do it anymore, yet is just as damned as an enemy, but at least he left saying that the message was right.

270.   I did not look for him; we met by chance on the street. If you choose to leave, do not expect me to beg you to return; you have lost, not me. If you leave, you are not one of us, so there is no reason I would want you back. I want people to have salvation and be happy and content with the Lord, but if you are not, I can do nothing except preach God's word.

271.   2 Corinthians 4:3 says,

3 But if our gospel be hid, it is hid to them that are lost:

References

1.   1. PCStudy Bible, Electronic Database. 1996 Biblesoft
2.   2. Ibid.
3.   3. Ibid.
4.   4. Ibid.
5.   5. Ibid.
6.   6. Ibid.
7.   7. Houghton Mifflin Company 1984, Websters's II New Riverside Dictionary. Berkley Books.
8.   8. PCStudy Bible, Electronic Database. 1996 Biblesoft
9.   9. Ibid.
10.   10. From International Standard Bible Encyclopaedia, Electronic Database Copyright © 1996 by Biblesoft
11.   11. PCStudy Bible, Electronic Database. 1996 Biblesoft
12.   12. Ibid.
13.   13. Ibid.
14.   14. Ibid.
15.   15. Ibid.
16.   16. Ibid.
17.   17. Ibid.
18.   18. Ibid.
19.   19. Ibid.
20.   20. Ibid.
21.   21. Ibid.

Chapter Two

Five Enlightenments

1. This Bible is Jesus and the body of Christ in a dehydrated form.

2. John 1:14 says,

14 And the Word was made flesh, and dwelt among us, and we beheld his glory, the glory as of the only begotten of the Father, full of grace and truth.

3. In other words, before Jesus was born, the Word was with God; it was not in the Bible.

4. John 1:1 says,

1 In the beginning was the Word, and the Word was with God, and the Word was God.

5. God's word became Christ when he was born; God created a human tabernacle, or a tent of flesh, and jumped into it.

6. John 17:5 says,

5 And now, O Father, glorify thou me with thine own self with the glory which I had with thee before the world was.

7. In the beginning, he was the word.

8. Matthew 26:26 says,

26 And as they were eating, Jesus took bread, and blessed it, and brake it, and gave it to the disciples, and said, Take, eat; this is my body.

9. The Catholic Church may have some truths, but they miss Jesus' meaning when he used bread as a symbolic representation of the word. In keeping with their doctrine of transubstantiation, the Catholic Church uses a wafer; the priest says hocus-pocus over it, and they believe that the wafer turns into the body of Jesus.

10. However, Jesus said his words were the bread of life. After Christ died, God dissolved him and returned him to be the Word, which is what he was in the beginning. Next, he put the word into a book we know as our Bible - the ink and paper of our Bible is Jesus Christ, or the nature of God, in dehydrated form.

11. The Bible is just a book of leather, paper, and ink, but when we hear it taught, understand it, and mix it with faith, it reacts like a package of dehydrated vegetables when we add water. The vegetables return to their original form.

12. Similarly, the word of God becomes what it was when Christ was here; it becomes the word made flesh, so when you hold the Bible in your hands, you are holding the K-rations or the dehydrated food of Jesus Christ. The word springs back to life when you hear a man of God teach it and understand it; every word of the Bible is a little piece of Jesus Christ.

13. Sometimes, when you put something on a cracker, it breaks apart, so you put those pieces on another.

Likewise, each word of the Bible is a crumb or a piece of Jesus Christ. Once you hear the word and mix it with faith, it comes back to life.

14. A Vacuum Sealer is an appliance used to remove air from food packages. In one television ad, they removed air from a bag of popcorn, which shrank to almost nothing. When they allowed air to return, it sprung to its original size.

15. There is a similar appliance that removes air to shrink pillows. When they allow air to return, the pillow inflates to its original size and form. The word of God works in the same manner. God shrunk or dehydrated the word and placed it into a book for us to eat.

16. Eating the word means hearing it taught. When you hear the word taught, you taste the word. You do not taste it with your physical tongue. You taste it with your ears because *"food for thought"* comes through the ears, not through the mouth.

17. Ephesians 3:17 says,

17 That Christ may dwell in your hearts by faith; that ye, being rooted and grounded in love,

18. Christ gets in you through teaching, hearing, and understanding.

19. 2 Corinthians 5:7 says,

7 For we walk by faith, not by sight:

20. And Hebrews 6:4 says,

4 For it is impossible for those who were <u>once</u> <u>enlightened</u>, and have tasted of the heavenly gift, and were made partakers of the Holy Ghost,

New Birth

21. Strong's definition of the word "once" is [1]

530 hapax hap'-ax;

- *probably from 537; one or a single time numerically or conclusively:*

22. You can only go to God once for your new birth or enlightenment. All of us will fall and make many mistakes in our lives, for which God has already forgiven us. Hebrews 6:4 is not talking about a minor mistake you did not mean to make; it is talking about coming to the knowledge of the truth that happens only once in your lifetime.

23. If you attend false churches, God will never enlighten you, no matter how much religious training you receive. Enlightenment can only take place in an authentic house of God. Enlightenment happens when you suddenly notice that you understand things about the Bible you never understood before.

24. Some may have attended my church and did not believe or agree with everything I taught, but eventually, they found themselves on my side and defended the message when they heard someone say

something contrary to what I taught. This person is rooted, grounded, and enlightened.

25. Jude 1:3 says,

3 Beloved, when I gave all diligence to write unto you of the common salvation, it was needful for me to write unto you, and exhort you that ye should earnestly contend for the faith which was <u>once</u> delivered unto the saints.

26. If God delivered the truth to you, he does not deliver it more than once. You may have to hear five hundred sermons before you get it, but once you get it, you are enlightened.

27. Again, Hebrews 6:4 says,

4 For it is impossible for those who were <u>once</u> <u>enlightened</u>, and have tasted of the heavenly gift, and were made partakers of the Holy Ghost,

28. It does not say twenty-five times that once is all it takes. Right now, I want to deal with something positive; I will start with *"once enlightened."*

Two Things

29. 1 Corinthians 1:25 says,

25 Because the foolishness of God is wiser than men; and the weakness of God is stronger than men.

30. God's weakness is better than us. Most churches preach lies about these two subjects. The first is that

nothing is impossible for God. The second is that God has no weakness, and he is all-powerful. These are both lies.

31. Hebrews 6:18 says,

18 That by two immutable things, in which it was impossible for God to lie, we might have a strong consolation, who have fled for refuge to lay hold upon the hope set before us:

32. It is impossible for God to lie, and it is impossible for God to restore those who walk away. God must have a weakness if he said his weakness is stronger than man. We know that God's weakness is the church, which is his wife. Adam's weakness was Eve, so a man's weakness is his woman; the weakness of God is the church.

33. I thank God that he said one of the things he cannot do is lie. Hebrews 6:18 says that God cannot lie, which means that God explicitly cannot lie to the brethren or church. I Kings 22:20-22 says some spirits would lie for God, so technically, if God sent a spirit to lie for him, he lied too, but he will not lie to his chosen church.

34. For example, he did not keep any secrets from Adam. When the voice of the Lord walked in the garden in the cool of the day, he was there to tell Adam the fullness of all things, but Satan had already deceived Eve, who gave to Adam, causing the voice of the Lord not to reveal what he planned to tell Adam.

35. John 10:27-28 says,

71

27 My sheep hear my voice, and I know them, and they follow me:

28 And I give unto them eternal life; and they shall never perish, neither shall any man pluck them out of my hand.

36. You cannot (and will not) walk away from the message if you are God's chosen, so if you can, God never called or chose you.

37. 1 John 2:19 says,

19 They went out from us, but they were not of us; for if they had been of us, they would no doubt have continued with us: but they went out, that they might be made manifest that they were not all of us.

38. If you attended a false church and later quit, you did not leave the true message of Jesus Christ. I left many churches in my life. False churches cannot enlighten us. A building with a sign naming it a church does not mean it is of God.

39. A chosen son of God will hear and understand the true message of Jesus Christ. Sons of God cannot walk away from the message. For example, Adam did not walk from God because 1 Timothy 2:14 says he was not in the transgression.

40. 1 Timothy 2:14 says,

14 And Adam was not deceived, but the woman being deceived was in the transgression.

41. We know that Adam physically left the garden, which means he walked away from the presence of God, but the Bible says that he was not in the transgression, which means God did not hold him accountable for that action.

42. It does not matter what our eyes see; only what God says is true, which mirrors the grace message I teach. It does not matter what people see our flesh do because if we are born of God, the real us (our inward man) cannot sin no matter what our fleshly bodies do.

43. 1 John 3:9 says,

9 Whosoever is born of God doth not commit sin; for his seed remaineth in him: and he cannot sin, because he is born of God.

44. Even though Adam physically walked away from God, God said he did not walk away. If you are God's child, you will never walk away from this enlightenment. You will never walk away from his true church because this is where the light is shining.

45. If you walk away from this true church, you damn yourself. If you can walk away from this church, you are not God's chosen. Someone in the world may be listening to me on the radio or on the Internet who is a son of God, but they do not know it yet. They may listen tonight and then not listen again for two years, but this message will stick with them.

46. Eventually, if they are sons of God, they will listen again and more often. Even though they may initially be adamant that they will never be a part of the

message, without realizing it, they become hooked; the message of truth will captivate God's chosen.

47. Those who are not God's chosen may stay in the message for years, playing the role of a son of God by listening and attending, but eventually, they will walk away. John 10:27-28 says that no man will pluck his sheep from his hand, so if you leave, you are not God's chosen.

48. Again, Hebrews 6:4 says,

4 For it is impossible for those who were <u>once</u> <u>enlightened</u>, and have tasted of the heavenly gift, and were made partakers of the Holy Ghost,

49. I know there are two things God cannot do because he said that he could not do them, yet some believe that God can do anything. Remember that the Bible says God cannot do these two things; I am not saying it.

50. Many ministers do not want to admit that there is something God cannot do. If God says it, that makes it so. He did not say that one of the things he could not do was to save adulterers, cheaters, murderers, or even a person as low as Hitler, but God did say that if he gave someone a chance at truth and they turn from it, he could not save them. That is a very powerful statement.

51. We think murderers, rapists, child molesters, and false churches should be at the top of the list, but God said the two things he cannot do is restore someone that has had the truth and then walk away and lie.

Be Adamant

52. Romans 8:35-36 says,

35 Who shall separate us from the love of Christ? shall tribulation, or distress, or persecution, or famine, or nakedness, or peril, or sword?

36 As it is written, For thy sake we are killed all the day long; we are accounted as sheep for the slaughter.

53. We must be as adamant as Paul is in Romans 8:35-36 because if you stay out of church for a weekend, you have committed a severe sin, and if you get mad at the preacher and decide to follow yourself, you have committed a grave sin.

54. Serving God is the most serious decision you will ever make; it is so severe that if you leave, you shut eternity's door on yourself. Many who leave blame everyone else but themselves. They blame the people in the congregation, they blame the man of God, or they blame circumstances.

55. They often say that the man of God did not understand their circumstance or dilemma, but the fact is that the problem was with them because they are not sons of God. I know this because others in the congregation have problems, and they are making it.

Once Enlightened

56. Again, Hebrews 6:4-6 says,

4 For it is impossible for those who were <u>once</u> <u>enlightened</u>, and have tasted of the heavenly gift, and were made partakers of the Holy Ghost,

5 And have tasted the good word of God, and the powers of the world to come,

6 If they shall fall away, to renew them again unto repentance; seeing they crucify to themselves the Son of God afresh, and put him to an open shame.

57. If you have one of the five things listed in Hebrews 6:4-5 but then commit the four things listed in Hebrews 6:6, you damn yourself.

58. Strong's definition of the word "enlightened" is [2]

5461 photizo fo-tid'-zo;

- *from 5457; <u>to shed rays</u>, i.e. to shine or transitively to brighten up literally or figuratively:*

KJV-- enlighten, illuminate, bring to, give light, make to see.

59. The word of God does not say that you must see all the word for him to enlighten you because enlightened means to shed rays.

60. According to Webster's II New Riverside Dictionary, the definition of the word "ray" is [3]

- *A thin line or narrow beam of radiation, esp. visible light.*

- *A small amount: trace.*

- *A ray of light is a small trace.*

61. John 8:12 says,

12 Then spake Jesus again unto them, saying, <u>I am the light of the world</u>: he that followeth me shall not walk in darkness, but shall have the light of life.

62. If you see a slight trace of light the size of a grain of mustard seed, it is bright enough to remove darkness. For example, if I shut off all the lights in this room, it would be pitch dark. Next, if I flick a cigarette lighter, I could take that little lighter and chase darkness all over the room.

63. Therefore, you do not have to see all the light; you only need to see a trace. When you see a ray of light from the sun shine through the clouds and the trees standing in the way, you do not see the sun's full impact, only a ray of the sun.

64. It is the same when you hear God's word. When you see a ray of God's word, you are accountable. Enlightened also means to shine or brighten up. It does not mean the brightest. It just means you begin to see some truth. You brighten up as you see the truth because you understand more than before hearing it.

65. Enlighten also means to illuminate and to be made to see. If you are in the message, and God's word is illuminated, brightens, or totally enlightens you, then you are accountable. If you are God's chosen, you will

stay faithful. Even if you are not God's chosen, you are accountable if you only receive a ray.

66. You must follow the message to obey it; if you do not follow the light, you make yourself twofold more a child of hell than you were before (Matthew 23:15). Remember that before you hear the true message of Jesus Christ you are lost, cut off from God and a sinner.

67. Those who do not hear the truth are lost, and God will punish them for their sins because of Adam, but those who received a ray of light and walked away will have a more severe punishment. Therefore, if you leave the truth after God enlightens you, you have turned from it, causing you to become a damned sinner, lost, and receive a harsher punishment than a person who has never walked into a house of God, having a chance to hear the word.

68. 2 Thessalonians 2:11-12 says,

11 And for this cause God shall send them strong delusion, that they should believe a lie:

12 That they all might be damned who believed not the truth, but had pleasure in unrighteousness.

69. Those who attend this church after being lost but walk away after receiving a ray of light damn and curse themselves! Also, whatever torments God issues at the White Throne Judgment will be more severe on those who have tasted the word or had a ray of light but then walked away from it than the torments God imposes on those who never tasted.

78

70. James 4:17 says,

17 Therefore to him that knoweth to <u>do good</u>, and doeth it not, to him it is sin.

71. And Matthew 19:17 says,

17 And he said unto him, Why callest thou me good? <u>there is none good but one, that is, God</u>: but if thou wilt enter into life, keep the commandments.

72. The wages of sin is death (Romans 6:23), and actual death is when God cuts you off from him. People out in the world are merely lost and unbelievers, but after they hear the truth and God enlightens them, they are now accountable and will receive more severe punishment if they walk away than if they had not heard.

73. 2 Peter 2:20 says,

20 For if after they have escaped the pollutions of the world through the knowledge of the Lord and Saviour Jesus Christ, they are again entangled therein, and overcome, the latter end is worse with them than the beginning.

74. Before people attend this church, they are just sinners out in the word, but after they acknowledge the truth by their continued presence, giving and agreeing with the message taught by saying Amen, they are accountable.

75. Simply saying Amen in this Church is very serious because you acknowledge that a ray of light hit you. If

you say Amen about something I already taught, you acknowledge that God enlightened you, so every time people nod their heads, say Amen, and attend a service, they acknowledge that God enlightened them, which means they are accountable.

76. God's word is much more serious than people think. For many years, I have warned that if people are not interested in truth, it is better for them not to walk through the doors of this ministry because they will hear me teach the truth. Enemies attended my ministry and agreed with what I taught, which means they are now accountable, so attending church is more than wearing nice clothes and saying, Hallelujah.

77. 1 Peter 4:17 says,

17 For the time is come that judgment must begin at the house of God: and if it first begin at us, what shall the end be of them that obey not the gospel of God?

78. If you attend this ministry, your judgment is happening now; when you acknowledge that something I teach is correct, you become accountable. You do not have to understand the entire Bible; you only need to receive a ray of truth for God to enlighten you. God shined his word upon you and illuminated you, which means you see him face to face. If God allows you to see him face to face, you must take it seriously. He did not even allow Moses to see him face to face. God only allowed Moses to see his back parts (Exodus 33:17-23).

79. 1 Corinthians 13:12 says,

12 For now we see through a glass, darkly; <u>but then</u>
<u>face to face</u>: now I know in part; but then shall I
know even as also I am known.

80. If God allows us to see him face to face, it is a very
serious matter because he allows us to see him as he is.
Paul could only see God through a glass darkly.
Hearing the word taught by a man of God is the only
way God will illuminate you. The Bible is a book of
darkness until the man of God picks up a spiritual
flashlight and shines on it.

81. Many think they can read the Bible themselves and
receive salvation, but that is the same as having a
flashlight with no batteries. The light will not come on
until you put the batteries in it; the bulb represents
God, and the batteries represent the man of God
teaching the word, which means you must have a
preacher.

82. Romans 10:14 says,

14 How then shall they call on him in whom they
have not believed? and how shall they believe in him
of whom they have not heard? and how shall they
hear without a preacher?

83. Symbolically, only the man of God can turn on the
flashlight. It is true that if you attended a false church,
you may hear something correct, but you will not hear
the truth because leaven contaminates it.

84. Galatians 5:9 says,

9 A little leaven leaveneth the whole lump.

85. Even though false churches might have one or two correct doctrines, the rest is full of error, contaminating what little truth they teach, but if you attend a church that teaches the truth of God's word and see just a tiny ray of light, the light you see is pure and uncontaminated.

Tasted of the Heavenly Gift
86. Again, Hebrews 6:4-6 says,

4 For it is impossible for those who were once enlightened, <u>and have tasted of the heavenly gift</u>, and were made partakers of the Holy Ghost,

5 And have tasted the good word of God, and the powers of the world to come,

6 If they shall fall away, to renew them again unto repentance; seeing they crucify to themselves the Son of God afresh, and put him to an open shame.

87. Strongs' definition of the phrase "have tasted" is [4]

1089 geuomai ghyoo'-om-ahee;

- *a primary verb; to taste; by implication, to eat; figuratively, to experience good or ill:*

88. And Thayers' definition of the phrase "have tasted" is [5]

1089 geuomai-

- *to taste, to try the flavor of*

- *to taste*
- *that is, perceive the flavor of, partake of, enjoy*
- *to feel, to make trial of, to experience*
- *to take food, eat, to take nourishment, eat*

89. Baskin & Robbins has 31 flavors of ice cream, but Religion has thousands of flavors in America alone! You may have tried one. Some of their names are Baptist, Catholic, and Methodist. When chosen, children of God hear the truth preached; a spark from a flinty rock will get their attention more than any other church they have attended.

90. However, when those who are lost see a spark from the flinty rock, they will say they cannot take it because they are Baptist through and through. When a saint sees the spark from the flinty rock, they will say it is the 32nd flavor they have been looking for; they heard the truth and have tasted the heavenly gift.

91. Romans 6:23 says,

23 For the wages of sin is death; but the gift of God is eternal life through Jesus Christ our Lord.

92. God's chosen will hear the message of eternity. Many have attended my church over the years; some stayed for ten years or more, but over time, they became used to the flavor until it suddenly tasted bad, even though it had been good for the past ten years.

93. It may not taste good to them anymore because of how I talk or dress or the length of my hair. It may also be that I rebuked someone but did not rebuke another

when they expected it. We must let God be God. There may be an instance where two people do the same thing wrong, but I may only rebuke one because I only chasten someone when God tells me.

94. It is very dangerous to attend a false church because you can get used to any flavor if you are around it long enough. For example, the first time most people taste a beer, they do not like it and cannot understand why anyone would drink it, but the more often they drink it, the more they get a taste for it.

95. Similarly, if you are around the Baptist church long enough, you will get a taste for it, so if genuine children of God attend a false church for most of their lives, they may get a taste for it. However, once they hear the truth, they will hunger for the real meat of God and not the vomit that the false church fed them.

96. Isaiah 28:7-8 says,

7 But they also have erred through wine, and through strong drink are out of the way; the priest and the prophet have erred through strong drink, they are swallowed up of wine, they are out of the way through strong drink; they err in vision, they stumble in judgment.

8 For all tables are full of vomit and filthiness, so that there is no place clean.

97. When you try a flavor, you perceive it. Sometimes, smelling food is like tasting. You can smell food cooking and get a taste in your mouth for it. Half the fun of eating a delicious meal is smelling the aroma in

the kitchen, but some must sniff very hard in our day because the cook is getting dinner out of a can.

98. In the old days, people cooked biscuits, gravy, fried food, and charcoal steaks, which smelled good. In comparison, when people first hear the truth, it smells good, even if they are not children of God.

99. Everyone who left this ministry stayed for a different length of time; one person lasted twenty-six years, while others only lasted one weekend before leaving. If they lasted long enough to say they did not like the message, then they have tasted it and have heard enough for the message to judge them.

100. If someone hears this message but rejects it, it does not mean the message is wrong; if you hear enough of this message that it grabs your attention to the point that you listened more than once, you are accountable, even if you do not agree with everything you heard.

101. 2 Peter 2:21 says,

21 For it had been better for them not to have known the way of righteousness, than, after they have known it, to turn from the holy commandment delivered unto them.

102. Smelling and eating literal food symbolizes how we taste spiritual food, which you do by hearing the word with your ears. Hearing is very powerful and subjective. I teach in a way that everyone will understand, so I use basic analogies like food and sex.

103.   A sexual encounter should begin when you get up in the morning, not after you get home from work. By making a phone call in the morning or making a suggestive comment to your significant other, you start the sexual process.

104.   The tone of your voice could decide the type of sexuality you manifest.   For example, you could whisper low and sultry in the other's ear or be more aggressive and get right in their ear.   The things you say can create a sexual atmosphere for later that day; of course, there are other ways to begin the sexual process, but one way is vocal.   Similarly, faith comes by hearing, so how you taste God's word is by hearing.

105.   Revelation 2:7 says,

*7 **He that hath an ear, let him hear what the Spirit saith unto the churches**; To him that overcometh will I give to eat of the tree of life, which is in the midst of the paradise of God.*

106.   And 1 Corinthians 2:14 says,

*14 But the natural man receiveth not the things of the Spirit of God: for they are foolishness unto him: neither can he know them, because **they are spiritually discerned**.*

107.   The natural man will never understand the Bible or why God does things the way he does, but the spiritual man will understand.   God convinced my congregation that there is an eternity and that he oversees it, so God illuminated his word and gave

them, at the very least, a ray of light, but God also gives enough light to unbelievers to hold them accountable.

Partakers of the Holy Ghost

108.   Again, Hebrews 6:4-6 says,

4 For it is impossible for those who were once enlightened, and have tasted of the heavenly gift, <u>and were made partakers of the Holy Ghost</u>,

5 And have tasted the good word of God, and the powers of the world to come,

6 If they shall fall away, to renew them again unto repentance; seeing they crucify to themselves the Son of God afresh, and put him to an open shame.

109.   Many believe you must speak in tongues to partake of the Holy Ghost. 1 Corinthians 12:9-10 lists nine gifts, and the gift of tongues and interpretation of tongues are last. They emphasize one gift only, even though there are nine.

110.   Strongs' definition of the word "partaker" is [6]

3353 metochos met'-okh-os;

* *from 3348; participant, i.e. as noun a sharer; by implication an associate:*

111.   To partake does not mean you must know everything about the Holy Ghost; it means you are a participant of the Holy Ghost. If you believe in a Holy

Ghost and hear the truth through him, then your ability to hear the truth means you have been in his presence.

112.   By hearing the truth, you become a partaker of the Holy Ghost because you cannot see the truth without partaking of the Holy Ghost; you can see the truth without the Holy Ghost filling you, but you cannot see the truth without at least partaking of the Holy Ghost because he is the spirit of truth. You can have rays of truth shine on you without the Holy Ghost filling you, but once he fills you, you will want him to lead you because the Holy Ghost will guide you into all truth.

113.   John 16:13 says,

13 Howbeit when he, the Spirit of truth, is come, he will guide you into all truth: for he shall not speak of himself; but whatsoever he shall hear, that shall he speak: and he will shew you things to come.

114.   To partake of the Holy Ghost, you must attend a church that teaches the truth. In such a church, you may receive a few rays to see if you will become hooked on the truth. You are accountable once you partake of the Holy Ghost and see some truth. How you worship God is essential because he wants people to worship him in spirit and in truth. He does not want people to worship him just for the sake of worshipping him.

Tasted the Good Word of God
115.   Again, Hebrews 6:4-6 says,

4 For it is impossible for those who were once enlightened, and have tasted of the heavenly gift, and were made partakers of the Holy Ghost,

5 <u>And have tasted the good word of God</u>, and the powers of the world to come,

6 If they shall fall away, to renew them again unto repentance; seeing they crucify to themselves the Son of God afresh, and put him to an open shame.

116.   Again, Strongs' definition of the phrase "have tasted" is [7]

1089 geuomai ghyoo'-om-ahee;

- *a primary verb; to taste; by implication, to eat; figuratively, to experience good or ill:*

117.   And, Thayers' definition of the phrase "have tasted" is [8]

1089 geuomai-

- *to taste, to try the flavor of*
- *to taste*
- *that is, perceive the flavor of, partake of, enjoy*
- *to feel, to make trial of, to experience*
- *to take food, eat, to take nourishment, eat*

118.   Tasting the heavenly gift means that you had some sight into eternity. You taste the good word of God by hearing the word taught and perceiving at least some of the truth it brings. When you taste the truth,

you learn about the Bible. Some do not listen to my teaching regularly because they disagree with it, but they will say I have some excellent points, so I have shed a ray on them, which means they are accountable.

Powers of the World to Come

119.   Again, Hebrews 6:4-6 says,

4 For it is impossible for those who were once enlightened, and have tasted of the heavenly gift, and were made partakers of the Holy Ghost,

5 And have tasted the good word of God, <u>and the</u> <u>powers of the world to come,</u>

6 If they shall fall away, to renew them again unto repentance; seeing they crucify to themselves the Son of God afresh, and put him to an open shame.

120.   Strongs' definition of the word "power" is [9]

1411 dunamis doo'-nam-is;

- *from 1410; force literally or figuratively; specially, miraculous power usually by implication, a miracle itself:*

KJV-- ability, abundance, meaning, might -ily, -y, -y deed, worker of miracle -s, power, strength, violence, mighty wonderful work.

121.   The word dynamite comes from the word dunamis.   Power also means force.   Romans 1:16 explains the power of God,

16 For I am not ashamed of <u>the gospel of Christ</u>: for it is the power of God unto salvation to every one that believeth; to the Jew first, and also to the Greek.

122.   If you sit on a stick of dynamite and light it, you can sing at the top of your lungs, "I shall not be moved," but when the dynamite explodes, you will move. Some do not believe everything I teach. They believe they do not have to obey everything the Bible says, but the Bible is the dunamis of God, so it will either blast you into salvation or damnation.

123.   The Bible is force, violence, and power. You cannot allow a powerful, violent, exploding force into your mind without something happening. It will either be positive or negative, but if you hear and understand at least some of the true message of Jesus Christ, something will happen in your life.

124.   Sometimes, when people attend this ministry, bad things happen, which contradicts the common belief that everything in your life is perfect when you have God. They do not understand that you are in a war zone when you are in God's real church. The truth is that things are getting better because you are finally in the real fight.

125.   Before someone starts attending God's real church, they are not even in the fight. Satan destroyed them because they could not fight back, but the more battles you fight, the stronger you become. Pretty soon, you have enough dunamis to handle the battles instead of the battles handling you.

126.   For example, we knew some things before school, but as we learn more about a subject, we gain more understanding. That gives us a greater ability in that field. The word of God works the same. After you gain knowledge of God's word, it begins to work and explode in your life. You become stronger and stronger until you reach a point where you love the battles, and you are even more determined not to give up.

127.   The biggest lie the devil is that if you do not go to church, you will have more money. I have proof that it is a lie. I have talked to people who have left this ministry and confessed believing they would have more money after leaving but ended up with less money than ever.

128.   It happens because life has a way of eating away at your money. When people walk away from God, they begin to live after their own decisions and lusts that eat away at their money without them knowing it.

129.   You only know that a fight is going on if you are in God. If you are not attending a true church of God, then you are unaware that there is a fight or that Satan is attacking and destroying you daily.

130.   The dunamis of the world to come means the power of eternity. If God does not extend time, we will all meet the graveyard head-on. There must be something more than this life. We live for about seventy years and die just as our intelligence peaks.

131.   If you believe there is something more than this life, you must do something about it. If you do nothing, the power of the world to come will make you explode. If you believe in the power of the world to come, and you see it through God's word, you are accountable.

132.   The five things listed in Hebrews 6:4-5 are: to be enlightened; tasted of the heavenly gift; made partakers of the Holy Ghost; have tasted the good word of God; and the powers of the world to come.

133.   After you experience the five things in your life spoken of in Hebrews 6:4-5, but then fall away, you put Jesus Christ to an open shame, and he will never renew you; if you have experienced any one of the five things, then you experienced all of them because they go together.

134.   Everyone in my congregation and those who listen to me on the radio or the internet have experienced at least one of the five things mentioned. I know some ministers do not agree with me, but they listen to my teaching to get help for their sermons. God is recording what they do because they are stealing from me. Since they get knowledge and understanding from me, they unwittingly allow rays of light to shine on them. They do not know what they have just done. He that hath ears let him hear what the Spirit says to the church.

135.   Deciding to serve God or coming to the house of God is the most critical decision you will ever make because it has eternal consequences. Some of us have made stupid decisions during our teenage years or

twenties. Now that we are in our forties, we still pay for those decisions. It does get better, but we must wait until our fifties.

136. Attending Church is not a game because eternal consequences are involved, unlike our flesh life. If every preacher taught this message fervently and plainly, more dedicated people would attend their churches instead of those who prefer to play games; I ensure my congregation knows how serious it is.

References

1. PCStudy Bible, Electronic Database. 1996 Biblesoft
2. Ibid.
3. Houghton Mifflin Company 1984, Webster's II New Riverside Dictionary. Houghton Mifflin Company, Massachusettes. Pg 580

4. PCStudy Bible, Electronic Database. 1996 Biblesoft
5. Ibid.
6. Ibid.
7. Ibid.
8. Ibid.
9. Ibid.

Chapter Three

Defining Hebrews 10:25

1. I have focused on the sixth chapter of Hebrews, but no matter which chapter of Hebrews I teach from, it is still the same book or letter. When he wrote this letter, Paul did not put in chapters and verses; a French monk who traveled from city to city on horseback put chapters and verses in the Bible. During his travels, he divided each book into chapters and verses so that it would be easier to find a topic instead of searching the whole letter when he taught.

2. I believe God directed him to do this, and he did it the way God wanted it done, but you must remember that when you read a book or letter and see a new chapter, it is not a new beginning; it is the same letter, so I believe God put in every coma, semicolon and period to signify a break.

3. Even though God added chapters and verses for our benefit, we must remember that when Paul wrote this letter, he wrote it as a continual chain of thought, so in the sixth chapter of Hebrews, Paul says that there are two things God cannot do; nothing and no one can limit God, but he did limit himself.

4. The first thing is that God cannot lie, and the second thing is that he cannot restore someone who has partaken of the truth of God's word but then walks away from it. It is better not to know God than to know even a small measure and not continue. For anyone who does this, their latter end will be worse than their beginning.

5. It is like dieting. You relax and let your guard down when you lose five or ten pounds. Soon after, you eat the same things you did before, which causes you to gain not only what you lost but also an added five or ten pounds from where you started. You would have been better off not dieting in the first place because your latter end is now worse than your beginning.

6. It is also the same with bodybuilders. They work hard and eat more to make the muscles of their body increase in size and strength, but once they stop working out, they lose muscle tissue. Fat will replace muscle if they continue eating the same amount of food until it hangs off their body; they end up worse than when they started.

7. Similarly, it is better not to hear one message of the truth of God's word than to hear it but not walk in it. Why did God put these issues in the Bible? What are the issues within Hebrews10:25-26? I will analyze this subject more in-depth than ever because people have told me that what I am saying is wrong for years. Even though the Bible says it, they do not believe God means it that way, so I will let the Bible speak for itself.

8. Hebrews 10:25-26 says,

25 Not forsaking the assembling of ourselves together, as the manner of some is; but exhorting one another: and so much the more, as ye see the day approaching.

26 For if we sin wilfully after that we have received the knowledge of the truth, there remaineth no more sacrifice for sins,

9.   Hebrews 10:25-26 **does not** say that if you commit adultery twenty-five times, God will forgive you, but if you commit adultery twenty-seven times, you went too far because you show no remorse for your actions.

10. Hebrews 10:25-26 **does not** discuss the issues of murder, adultery, or any other fleshly sin. Consequently, these verses do not discuss murderers, adulterers, fornicators, strippers, prostitutes, or homosexuals.

11. These verses specifically talk about assembling ourselves with the body of Christ and with the correct attitude of worship, so God considers worshiping the highest act for which he holds us accountable.

12. God did not say that if you kill someone, there remaineth no more sacrifice for your sins, but he did say in Hebrews 10:25-26 that if you forsake the assembling of yourself together, there remaineth no more sacrifice for your sins, which is a very profound and powerful statement.

13. Someone who left this church told me that they did not believe Hebrews 10:26 had anything to do with Hebrews 10:25 because it discussed a completely different subject. If they have nothing to do with each other, why did Paul place Hebrews 10:26 right after Hebrews 10:25 instead of another part of the letter?

14. This person tried to wiggle out of Hebrews 10:26 because he decided within his pea-sized brain that there are worse sins than forsaking church assembly. That is not what the Bible says! If you believe otherwise, you are a hypocrite! I get mad when people defame the Bible! God is not stupid! He put Hebrews 10:26 after Hebrews 10:25 because he wanted it there.

15. When Paul wrote this letter to the Hebrews, he did not break it down by chapter and verse. Instead, he wrote these verses within the same paragraph, which means he continued the same thought from the prior sentence.

16. God did not put Hebrews 10:26 in the Ten Commandments, where he talked about murder and adultery. There is a reason God put Hebrews 10:26 where he did; one thing is sure: he did not put it there for us to ignore, as most churches do.

17. Luke 4:4 says,

4 And Jesus answered him, saying, It is written, That man shall not live by bread alone, but by every word of God.

18. And Matthew 4:4 says,

4 But he answered and said, It is written, Man shall not live by bread alone, but by every word that proceedeth out of the mouth of God.

19. And Deuteronomy 8:3 says,

3 And he humbled thee, and suffered thee to hunger, and fed thee with manna, which thou knewest not, neither did thy fathers know; that he might make thee know that man doth not live by bread only, but by every word that proceedeth out of the mouth of the LORD doth man live.

20. And 2 Timothy 3:16 says,

16 All scripture is given by inspiration of God, and is profitable for doctrine, for reproof, for correction, for instruction in righteousness:

21. It includes Hebrews 10:25-26.

22. 2 Peter 1:21 says,

21 For the prophecy came not in old time by the will of man: but holy men of God spake as they were moved by the Holy Ghost.

23. And Galatians 1:1 says,

1 Paul, an apostle, not of men, neither by man, but by Jesus Christ, and God the Father, who raised him from the dead;

Line in the Sand
24. Paul spoke it, and his letter is in the Bible, which means that Jesus said it through Paul. I consider all scripture in the Bible to be the words of Jesus; when Jesus was born, he was the word made flesh.

25. Again, why did God put Hebrews 10:26 right after Hebrews 10:25? In doing so, God drew a line in the

sands of time. Just like when we were younger and a fight was about to happen, we would draw a line in the dirt and tell the person not to cross that line. We hoped they would not cross it because we had to put up or shut up if they did.

26. Sometimes, we would draw another line if they crossed the first, and another if they crossed the second one, and so on. In the same respect, Jesus drew a line in the sands of time. We find that line in Hebrews 10:26 for our admonition.

27. Again, Hebrews 10:25-26 says,

25 Not forsaking the assembling of ourselves together, as the manner of some is; but exhorting one another: and so much the more, as ye see the day approaching.

26 For if we sin wilfully after that we have received the knowledge of the truth, there remaineth no more sacrifice for sins,

28. The argument begins with the opening words, Not forsaking the assembling. What is forsaking? Many believe that if they only miss one service, it does not mean they have forsaken God. It was an inconvenience, or they chose not to attend that day. They still claim to love and serve God. They just missed one service.

29. They believe that forsaking means quitting attending church altogether, not missing one service. In response, I will refer to God's word and the original language to determine what the word forsaking means.

101

Although they believe that missing one service does not mean they have forsaken God and truth, they did forsake that one service.

30. They forsook God for that moment or that atom of time, and if God's representative set up that moment or atom of time to dispense faith, they were not there to receive it. They may not have meant to forsake all of God, but they did forsake that daily bread moment.

31. Matthew 6:11 says,

11 Give us this day our daily bread.

32. Jesus drew a line in the sand and said that if you step over that line, there remaineth no more sacrifice for your sins, and you become an enemy of the cross.

33. Philippians 3:17-19 says,

17 Brethren, be followers together of me, and mark them which walk so as ye have us for an ensample.

18 For many walk, of whom I have told you often, and now tell you even weeping, that they are the enemies of the cross of Christ:

19 Whose end is destruction, whose God is their belly, and whose glory is in their shame, who mind earthly things.

34. We must decide whether Jesus was bluffing or really meant it when he drew a line in the sands of time. Will he draw another line if we cross it? And another?

And another? Will he back up, or will he stand firm? If he backs up, we do not have a dilemma.

35. We must figure out what forsaking means in God's view. We know that if we walk out of a store, it does not mean we are never coming back. It does not mean we have forsaken shopping there forever or that we will not return to the store any more today.

36. However, stores did not draw a line in the sand, saying that if you do not come today, you can never shop at this store again; they will let you come and go as you please. Conversely, God drew a line in the sand and said we could not come and go as we pleased. We cannot do things how or when we want to do them. We must do things God's way.

37. Matthew 6:33 says,

33 But seek ye first the kingdom of God, and his righteousness; and all these things shall be added unto you.

38. And Matthew 19:29 says,

29 And every one that hath forsaken houses, or brethren, or sisters, or father, or mother, or wife, or children, or lands, for my name's sake, shall receive an hundredfold, and shall inherit everlasting life.

39. Jesus taught emphatically that God and the Word must be first in your life, so since Jesus is the Word, he said he must be first in your life.

40. 1 Corinthians 6:19-20 says,

19 What? know ye not that your body is the temple of the Holy Ghost which is in you, which ye have of God, and ye are not your own?

20 For ye are bought with a price: therefore glorify God in your body, and in your spirit, which are God's.

41. And Luke 9:59-60 says,

59 And he said unto another, Follow me. But he said, Lord, suffer me first to go and bury my father.

60 Jesus said unto him, Let the dead bury their dead: but go thou and preach the kingdom of God.

Not Forsaking
42. Jesus laid out the principles of his intellect. We must study his intellect before knowing his definition of the word forsaking. In Luke 9:60, Jesus said, *"Let the dead bury their dead."* If you put him first, you must go now. Jesus told Peter to follow him. Peter was a fisherman and owned his own business, including fishing ships.

43. Jesus did not wait for Peter to be ready in his own good time, or when Peter decided it was the right thing to do; he told Peter to follow him, and he meant right away. Jesus did the same with Matthew, Mark, Luke, John, and all the other disciples. From Jesus' point of view, since he alone has the words of eternal life, nothing else matters.

44. Matthew 16:13-16 says,

13 When Jesus came into the coasts of Caesarea Philippi, he asked his disciples, saying, Whom do men say that I the Son of man am?

14 And they said, Some say that thou art John the Baptist: some, Elias; and others, Jeremias, or one of the prophets.

15 He saith unto them, But whom say ye that I am?

16 And Simon Peter answered and said, Thou art the Christ, the Son of the living God.

45. Jesus wanted to know who the disciples thought he was. Peter boldly spoke up and said that Jesus was the Christ, the son of the living God. Jesus told Peter that flesh and blood did not give that revelation to him; God did, and since Jesus was God in the flesh, everything he said was right. Moreover, nothing else matters since he alone has the words of eternal life.

46. Jesus expected Peter to follow and put him before his wife, job, and himself. Jesus expected everything in Peter's life to be less important than him at that moment and to follow him. Jesus wants to be first and reign supreme in your life. If you do not put him first in your life, he will cut you off and put someone else in your place who will put him first.

47. The theory that Jesus will compromise his spiritual laws because he understands you have problems is false. You do not have any more problems in your life than anyone else. The problems of our day move faster because we can access vehicles like cars and jets. We also have access to computers.

105

48. Our problems are the same as in the 1500s, except their issues moved slowly. Since they were human, they had the same troubles we do today. Jesus expected everyone to put him first and everything else second. Consequently, when Jesus said not forsaking, he did not mean that it is okay to miss once in a while, so long as you do not forsake him altogether. That does not sound like Jesus.

49. John 14:6 says,

6 Jesus saith unto him, I am the way, the truth, and the life: no man cometh unto the Father, but by me.

50. And Matthew 6:33 says,

33 But seek ye first the kingdom of God, and his righteousness; and all these things shall be added unto you.

51. And Matthew 19:29 says,

29 And every one that hath forsaken houses, or brethren, or sisters, or father, or mother, or wife, or children, or lands, for my name's sake, shall receive an hundredfold, and shall inherit everlasting life.

52. How can anyone read the prior verses and think that when he said, not forsaking, he only meant that you should not give up? That is someone willing to compromise. That is someone who understands and cares about your problems. That is someone who understands that there are certain things you must do in this life.

53. They believe they can miss church, not read, pray, or not arrive on time because things happen. They believe Jesus understands and everything will be all right, but only if you do not quit permanently. That is not the pattern Jesus laid out when he taught.

54. Again, John 14:6 says,

6 Jesus saith unto him, I am the way, the truth, and the life: no man cometh unto the Father, but by me.

55. And Luke 9:59-60 says,

59 And he said unto another, Follow me. But he said, Lord, suffer me first to go and bury my father.

60 Jesus said unto him, Let the dead bury their dead: but go thou and preach the kingdom of God.

56. Again, Jesus did not want that young man to go to his daddy's funeral because it would take too long, so if the young man wanted to follow him, he had to do it immediately. You must forsake your job, family, and everything to follow Jesus.

57. Again, how can anyone think that when Jesus said, "Not forsaking," he did not mean all the time? Some foolishly think he only means that we should not quit permanently and that it is acceptable to miss from time to time based on your circumstances. That does not sound right.

58. 1 Corinthians 7:22 says,

22 For he that is called in the Lord, being a servant, is the Lord's freeman: likewise also he that is called, being free, is Christ's servant.

59. You are the Lord's freeman. That is your circumstances. You do not own yourself; you do not belong to yourself; you do not own your career, and you cannot run your own life because you are the Lord's. You are at his service twenty-four hours a day. He allows you to have a life, but you must align it with his will.

The Man of Sin
60. 2 Thessalonians 2:3 says,

3 Let no man deceive you by any means: for that day shall not come, except there come a falling away first, and <u>that man of sin be revealed</u>, the son of perdition;

61. *"That man of sin be revealed"* shows you are a loser. You are a man of sin, and that new man within you must overpower your outer man and become more important. It is a revelation because most ministers teach that the man of sin is the antichrist. They believe that one day, God will reveal the antichrist; they are so busy looking for it that they miss who the man of sin is.

62. We live with the man of sin daily because he is the one who tells us that we have important things to do. He is the one who tells us that we can be late for church or miss one service, and it will not hurt. The man of sin does not want us to obey the word because he knows that obedience is better than sacrifice and that God expects us to obey.

63. 2 Thessalonians 2:3 says there must come a falling away first, so there will be a forsaking; if you do not obey every word of God, you have denied the word by falling prey to the man of sin, and you fell away.

64. 1 John 2:4 says,

4 He that saith, I know him, and keepeth not his commandments, is a liar, and the truth is not in him.

65. Many say they did not fall away from all of God but only from one word. That one word is all of God. One grain of mustard seed is all of God. You may have a barrel full of mustard seeds, but each one of those mustard seeds is all of God.

66. It is the same as taking a glass of water from the ocean. The glass does not hold the whole ocean, but if you analyze the ingredients of the water in the glass, it will match what is in the ocean, so as a result, if you disobey one word of God, you disobey God; if you disobey one word of God, you forsake God.

67. Psalms 119:89 says,

89 For ever, O LORD, thy word is settled in heaven.

68. What excuse could you have for missing a service?

69. Luke 14:17-20 says,

17 And sent his servant at supper time to say to them that were bidden, Come; for all things are now ready.

18 And they all with one consent began to make
excuse. The first said unto him, I have bought a piece
of ground, and I must needs go and see it: I pray thee
have me excused.

19 And another said, I have bought five yoke of oxen,
and I go to prove them: I pray thee have me excused.

20 And another said, I have married a wife, and
therefore I cannot come.

70. These people did not say they did not want to eat
supper, only that they could not attend that day. The
person mentioned in Luke 14:20 just married, so he
was on his honeymoon. Some think God will
understand if they are on their honeymoon because it
is a once-in-a-lifetime event.

71. Well, you never know; there could be many more
honeymoons in your future, but even if there are no
more, there are no scriptures in the Bible to support
that belief. The Bible says not to forsake the
assembling of yourselves together. Again, the issue
will be what people consider forsaking. These people
think missing one service is not forsaking because they
still love God.

72. 1 John 2:4 says,

4 He that saith, I know him, and keepeth not his
commandments, is a liar, and the truth is not in him.

73. They think they love God, but based on his
definition, they do not; our definition of love does not
matter. It is God's definition of love that counts. It

relates to my story about someone buying a loved one a birthday gift. The person having the birthday may tell them what they would like to receive, but instead, the person buying the gift gets something they want them to have instead of what the person wanted.

74. That type of person is not a true giver, and giving that gift was not an act of love. The person giving the gift satisfied himself or herself. If you find reasons not to keep the word, you are satisfying yourself, but the word is forever settled.

75. Exodus 32:26 says,

26 Then Moses stood in the gate of the camp, and said, Who is on the LORD's side? let him come unto me. And all the sons of Levi gathered themselves together unto him.

76. And 2 Thessalonians 2:11-12 says,

11 And for this cause God shall send them strong delusion, that they should believe a lie:

12 That they all might be damned who believed not the truth, but had pleasure in unrighteousness.

77. And 1 Corinthians 7:22-23 says,

22 For he that is called in the Lord, being a servant, is the Lord's freeman: likewise also he that is called, being free, is Christ's servant.

23 Ye are bought with a price; be not ye the servants of men.

78. If God called you, you are his servant. As his servant, your time is not your own because you are alive to serve him. Servants do not have a life outside their service. If they do, then they must put their life after their work. A servant is the Lord's freeman. You are free if you acknowledge he owns you. You are the Lord's freeman.

79. Again, 1 Corinthians 7:22 says, *"likewise also he that is called, being free, is Christ's servant."* This verse refers to those who obey the word. God bought you with a price, which means you are not a servant of men.

80. 1 Corinthians 6:19-20 says,

19 What? know ye not that your body is the temple of the Holy Ghost which is in you, which ye have of God, and ye are not your own?

20 For ye are bought with a price: therefore glorify God in your body, and in your spirit, which are God's.

81. Some say they will lose their jobs if they attend church all the time. You should consider it an honor to lose your job for obeying the written word because many lose their jobs over stupid crap. If you lost your job for obeying God's word and not because you were always late or lazy, it is a tremendous honor that you cannot buy with money. You would have a testimony that you were true to the word. If you lose your job because of obedience, you should thank God for being rid of that job.

82. Think about what God gave up for you. What if Jesus missed just one day of his calling? Jesus manifested God's word, name, and nature on earth for thirty-three and a half years. During the last three and a half years of his life, he preached at the temple and on the roads to Jerusalem, Bethlehem, and Judea.

83. He was on time when he talked to the woman at the well; he healed the sick, raised the dead, opened blind eyes, opened deaf ears, and spoke knowledge to the ignorant. He healed people with leprosy and a woman with an issue of blood. He was on time for each incident. When it was time to raise Lazarus from the dead, he was on time.

84. Some said he was late, but if Jesus had arrived before Lazarus died, he could not raise him from the dead. The point is that you should not be late for church and the worship of God because it would show that something else is important to you.

Being Late
85. Some are late for everything, even important things. They believe they are more important than anything else. It does not work that way here. What if Jesus believed that it would not hurt to miss a day? What if he decided to miss the day he destined himself to die for you and me? We would not have salvation for our sins.

86. Some argue that since the day he died was important, they will come to church if it is an essential service. Which message is more important than another? You are a hypocrite if you dare say to God

113

that one sermon is more important than another, so you can miss the one you think is unimportant.

87. Jesus performed many mighty miracles in his lifetime. He fed five thousand people, not counting women and children, with the miracle of the fish and loaves of bread. He healed many of their infirmities, opened blind eyes and deaf ears, and raised the dead.

88. However, only a few attended the service on the day Jesus died on the cross. Those who missed, which were many, did not say he was a devil and would not follow him; they had other things to do on that day. The Bible says he looked down from the cross and saw only a few supporters.

89. John 19:27 says,

27 Then saith he to the disciple, Behold thy mother! And from that hour that disciple took her unto his own home.

90. And John 6:66 says,

66 From that time many of his disciples went back, and walked no more with him.

91. What if Jesus missed a day during his ministry? Let us set aside the day Rome crucified him and examine the day he healed blind Bartimaeus. If Jesus had decided to take that day off, he would not have healed blind Bartimaeus; that day was a step Jesus needed to take to fulfill the crucifixion.

92. Had he taken that day off, he would not have been at the right place and time for the crucifixion. Instead, he would have arrived a few days or weeks later simply because he missed one day. What if Noah had taken one day off after one hundred twenty-five years of hard work? What if that day was the day God chose to shut the door to the ark? Some argue that God would not have shut the door if Noah was not there; the Bible says that no man could open the door after God shut it.

93. Some claim they would have been there that day because it was necessary. People who choose to miss services would not have known about the importance of that day because they would not have been there for the others. During the one hundred twenty-five years Noah preached that it would rain, he might have thought that every day could be the day.

94. What would he be doing daily? He would be doing his job. He would not miss a day because he had to put more nails in the ark and be there just in case. People who choose to miss services say that some of my sermons are important, but some are not, but my sermons are not the subject.

95. The issue is "not forsaking the assembling of yourselves together." Jesus did not forsake his calling. Paul was not late for his calling because he decided to take the day off. Peter, John, and Luke did not take the day off. Jehu and Gideon were there.

96. Jonah wanted to take a day off and miss one service in Nineveh. God did not allow him to miss it and forced him to go. Some counter by saying he was late getting to Nineveh because he went in the opposite

direction. That is wrong. He was not late because the sermon did not start until he arrived in Nineveh.

97. Hebrews 13:8 says,

8 Jesus Christ the same yesterday, and to day, and for ever.

98. They did not miss their appointments, so we should not miss ours either.

99. Matthew 24:44 says,

44 Therefore be ye also ready: for in such an hour as ye think not the Son of man cometh.

100.   You do not know which service it will be when I say the right word to start the explosion.

101.   Again, Hebrews 10:25 says,

25 Not forsaking the assembling of ourselves together, as the manner of some is; but exhorting one another: and so much the more, as ye see the day approaching.

102.   This verse means that you must get to church on time.   What is the whole point of assembling ourselves together? The first answer is that God said we must do it. The second answer is that if one child of God can put a thousand evil spirits to flight, then two can put ten thousand to flight. You are not assembling yourselves when you gather around the Internet or radio; you are only partially doing it.

103.   Hebrews 11:6 says,

6 But without faith it is impossible to please him: for he that cometh to God must believe that he is, and that he is a rewarder of them that diligently seek him.

104.   It does not matter if you wear a dress that extends to Baltimore. It does not matter if the women refrain from cutting or coloring their hair. Without faith, you cannot please God. You are not born with faith because faith comes by hearing the word of God, and Romans 10:13-15 tells us how to get that faith when it says,

13 For whosoever shall call upon the name of the Lord shall be saved.

14 How then shall they call on him in whom they have not believed? and how shall they believe in him of whom they have not heard? and how shall they hear without a preacher?

15 And how shall they preach, except they be sent? as it is written, How beautiful are the feet of them that preach the gospel of peace, and bring glad tidings of good things!

105.   If God tells the man of God to visit your house at every church service, then you could stay at home because he would dispense faith to you at your house, but when the man of God sets a time and a place for everyone to meet, you must be there.

106.   There were occasions in the Bible when the men of God went from house to house, but we have a

place to assemble ourselves together. Each person knows that the man of God has chosen each Friday, Saturday, and Sunday as the time we are to assemble ourselves together. The Bible says that you must have faith to please God. The man of God is the only one who can teach faith.

Gathered Together
107.   Luke 17:37 says,

37 And they answered and said unto him, Where, Lord? And he said unto them, Wheresoever the body is, thither will the eagles be gathered together.

108.   I have appointed times for us to meet. I will be here on Friday and Sunday, preaching God's word, so the eagles, which symbolize the body of Christ, should gather together where I am so that I can dispense faith to them.

109.   If you choose not to be here at those times, you have counted the faith of this day to be unimportant by your actions, proving you do not believe the Bible when it says that we must have bread given to us daily. Wherever the man of God is teaching is where you will get faith, which means you must also be there.

110.   Even if I am teaching over the radio, I am teaching faith. I am doing my part by providing it. After you hear faith taught, it should create a magnetic field in your spirit that will cause you to want to assemble yourself with the body of Christ. When I teach over the radio and the Internet, I am fishing. When a fisherman throws a net out into the ocean, he hopes to gather those fish into his boat.

118

111.   Spiritually, my net is the radio, internet, and recordings. Once the net catches some fish, I pull it into the boat to gather them together. If some fish do not come because they have escaped the net, they are not God's chosen. There is no way a fish can live in the net or on a hook; the point of throwing the net is to bring the fish in.

112.   God sends his word out through radio and the internet so people can learn to assemble themselves together. What you receive through radio, the internet, and recordings is a small taste. If you do not believe what you hear over the radio, you are damned because you reject God's word, even if it is a taste. What I teach over the radio should create a desire to assemble with the body of Christ.

113.   John 12:25-26 says,

25 He that loveth his life shall lose it; and he that hateth his life in this world shall keep it unto life eternal.

26 If any man serve me, let him follow me; and where I am, there shall also my servant be: if any man serve me, him will my Father honour.

114.   And Matthew 18:20 says,

20 For where two or three are gathered together in my name, there am I in the midst of them.

115.   God is everywhere, but his purpose is not everywhere, including weddings, anniversaries, jazz festivals, or the beach. God is everywhere, and if you

119

are there, he is there, but when the body of Christ gathers together, or even if two or three gather together, he said he is in the midst.

116.   Again, Jesus said in John 12:26 where I am, that is where you should follow, so if I am here and at least a couple more saints are here with me on Friday and Sunday, that is where you should be because this is where he is. God is everywhere, but he does not reveal himself everywhere. God does not show his face everywhere; he only shows his face where the body gathers together, and we can see him face to face.

117.   If I preach with two or more saints in attendance, those at a bar will not see God's face because he is not revealing himself there. Jesus is in the midst of the body of Christ, not in the midst of someone's family unless they are at a church that preaches truth; as some learn more about God, they sometimes discover that their earthly family is crazy.

118.   Romans 6:23 says,

23 For the wages of sin is death; but the gift of God is eternal life through Jesus Christ our Lord.

119.   You cannot get the gift of God through family, friends, jobs, or careers. You get the gift of God through Jesus Christ, who is here in the midst of the body of Christ. When God's children hear the truth taught, it will bring them in, but if some hear it and it reaches their hearts without feeling the urge to move and become part of the body of Christ, God will not save them. That is what the truth does.

120

120.   Jesus said that men of God are fishers of men. In Jesus' day, those who fished for a living did not throw any fish back into the water because it was not a sport to them; it was their livelihood. When I throw out the net, I expect to pull some in. Some who hear the word taught will only come in if they want. If their commitment   to   attending   church   becomes inconvenient to the others in the school of fish with whom they swim, they will not come because of peer pressure.

121.   If I hook them, but it is inconvenient for them on that day, they say, "You will have to wait; I cannot come today because I have things to do, but one day I will come." It does not work that way. You will come when the fisherman catches you by preaching the truth. You must be where the man of God dispenses faith.

122.   Grace covers the inherent sins of the flesh, but you can only get grace through faith. Faith comes by hearing the word of God taught by a preacher. The only place you can get faith is where a true man of God is teaching.

123.   If you want grace so the blood of Christ can cover the inherent sins of your flesh, you must have your body and mind at the place where the man of God is dispensing faith. It will allow faith to enter your inner man, producing grace to cover your outer man and enabling you to fully concentrate on your obedience to the word, not your life.

124.   1 Samuel 15:22 says,

22 And Samuel said, Hath the LORD as great delight in burnt offerings and sacrifices, as in obeying the voice of the LORD? Behold, to obey is better than sacrifice, and to hearken than the fat of rams.

125.   Grace will cover the sins of the outer man, but grace will not cover the sins of the inner man, which includes you forsaking the assembling together with the body of Christ.

126.   Hebrews 10:23 says,

23 Let us hold fast the profession of our faith without wavering; for he is faithful that promised;

127.   Once we have faith, we should not waiver or fall backward and forward. You do not have to waiver in faith because it is the word of God, and his word is forever settled. Some idiots said they would have to pray about the prior statement. There is nothing to pray about because faith does not come by praying; it comes by hearing the word of God taught.

128.   If you believe that the Bible is the word of God, then you must believe what I said. God does not waiver, which can be good and bad for us. God does not waiver on his promise that if you sin willfully, there are no more sacrifices for your sins.

So Much the More
129.   There are sixty-six books in the Bible, and one verse found in Hebrews 10:25 says,

25 Not forsaking the assembling of ourselves together, as the manner of some is; but exhorting one another: <u>and so much the more, as ye see the day approaching</u>.

130.　The defining phrase of Hebrews 10:25 is, *"and so much the more, as ye see the day approaching."* You cannot occasionally miss a service and, at the same time, do it *"so much the more."* I am on shortwave radio seven days a week and on the Internet twenty-four hours a day, so I have increased my broadcast.

131.　If I choose to have a service every night of the week and to make it mandatory for everyone to be here, the Bible supports my decision. I do not care about your career. Jesus did not refuse to bear the cross with the nails in his hands because he was a model, and it would ruin his skin. Some miss church because they have an appointment to get a skin treatment. What if Jesus refused to go to the cross because he became a model and would only go there after his modeling career?

132.　It is the same as people who studied all their lives for a particular career but would not give it up to be in the house of God when it became necessary. Before choosing a career, they should have asked God for direction rather than making their own choice. It is God's fault, not mine. Depending upon the situation, some may need to change their job or leave their wives or husbands.

133.　Romans 8:38-39 says,

38 For I am persuaded, that neither death, nor life, nor angels, nor principalities, nor powers, nor things present, nor things to come,

39 Nor height, nor depth, nor any other creature, shall be able to separate us from the love of God, which is in Christ Jesus our Lord.

134.   Some women say they cannot attend church because their husbands will not let them. Since God is your true husband, you should eliminate any man who would try to supersede God because that man is an idiot.

135.   Matthew 6:33 says,

33 But seek ye first the kingdom of God, and his righteousness; and all these things shall be added unto you.

136.   And Luke 9:59-60 says,

59 And he said unto another, Follow me. But he said, Lord, suffer me first to go and bury my father.

60 Jesus said unto him, Let the dead bury their dead: but go thou and preach the kingdom of God.

137.   Jesus did not care about the death of this man's father. The traditional churches of our day do not serve this God; they serve a sweet pea God who loves everyone and falls over himself at funerals because he cares so much. God is not like that.

138.   Many who claim to be Christians say they love God, yet they either do not attend church regularly or do not attend at all. If a person willfully misses a church service, they are exercising control over that event and have not put God first.

139.   You cannot control some circumstances, such as car accidents, hospitalization, physical incapacitation, or death. When some dedicated saints were in the hospital, they wanted to leave to be in church on time. I had to tell them to stay because they were too sick. That is how a true saint of God should react.

140.   Another example is if you drive to church during a snowstorm and there is an accident in your way that keeps you from getting to church. In that case, God does not hold you accountable because you had the will to get to church, so by your faith, God credits you as being there.

141.   Unacceptable excuses include working, feeling sick, tired, or having headaches from watching children all day. Other than severe illness, accidents, or death, I do not know of any excuses for missing a church service. If you miss for any other reason, you are putting God second.

142.   Hebrews 10:26 says,

26 For if we sin wilfully after that we have received the knowledge of the truth, there remaineth no more sacrifice for sins,

143.   If you sin willfully and forsake the assembling of yourselves together, you are under fiery judgment and damnation. The main issue for this subject will revolve around the definition of the word forsaking; people often argue that they did not forsake God because they only missed a service.

144.   Matthew 4:4 says,

4 But he answered and said, It is written, Man shall not live by bread alone, <u>but by every word</u> that proceedeth out of the mouth of God.

145.   And Matthew 6:33 says,

33 But seek ye first the kingdom of God, and his righteousness; and all these things shall be added unto you.

146.   Again, having to work, being tired, or having a headache are unacceptable excuses. Nor is it an acceptable excuse to skip church because your husband or wife will not let you attend.

Forsaking
147.   Strongs' definition of the word "forsaking" is [1]

5805 `azuwbah az-oo-baw';

- *feminine passive participle of 5800; <u>desertion</u> of inhabitants:*

148.   If you missed one service, you have *deserted* that service. What if Jesus deserted one day?

149.   Strongs' definition of the word "forsaken" is [2]

5800 `azab aw-zab';

- *a primitive root; to loosen, i.e. relinquish, permit, etc.:*

- *commitself, fail, forsake, fortify, help, leave destitute, off, refuse, X surely.*

150.   Brown-Driver-Brigg's definition of the word "forsaken" is [3],

5800 `azab-

- *to leave, to loose, to forsake*
- *Qal to leave*
- *to depart from, to leave behind, to leave, to let alone*
- *to leave, to abandon, to forsake, to neglect, to apostatize*
- *to let loose, to set free, to let go, to free*
- *Niphal*
- *to be left to*
- *to be forsaken*
- *Pual to be deserted*
- *to restore, to repair Qal*

151.   According to Roget's New Millennium™ Thesaurus, First Edition v 1.3.1 [4]

- *A synonym for the word "abandon" is interrupt.*

127

152.   You *permitted* yourself to miss one service, but God did not *permit* it. The word did not change; it stayed the same, but you *permitted* yourself to miss. If you missed church because your mother came to visit you on that day, you just *deserted* because you put your mother before your God. If you missed church to wax your car because it was a nice day, your car just became more important to you than Jesus.

153.   Again, Luke 9:59-60 says,

59 And he said unto another, Follow me. But he said, Lord, suffer me first to go and bury my father.

60 Jesus said unto him, Let the dead bury their dead: but go thou and preach the kingdom of God.

154.   At that moment, your car became more important to you than God because you *permitted* yourself to wax a piece of fiberglass rather than attend church, where you would have heard the words of eternal life preached, and you would have received faith. By your actions, you proclaimed that a wax job was more important to you than being in church.

155.   Matthew 6:21 says,

21 For where your treasure is, there will your heart be also.

156.   Forsaken also means to fail. If you miss a service, you fail on that day. Some skip church to attend their family reunion. Which family reunion is more important to you? Your heavenly family should be more important to you, yet some will say that since

128

they always go to church, it should not hurt to visit their natural family during a service occasionally.

157.   Jesus said to let the dead bury the dead, which shows the heart of the matter he was trying to convey. We must forsake all.   Why do they plan family reunions on church days?   Why do employers tempt you with overtime on Friday nights?

158.   You must understand that something is working behind the scenes, enticing you to break God's word. People will plan family reunions, high school reunions, birthday parties, weddings, ceremonies, and funerals at a time when it would interfere with your attendance in the house of God. Could this be a plot? Yes. God made Satan for the sole purpose of trying to make you break just one word of the bible because Satan knows that if you break one word, you are guilty of all of them.

159.   Forsaken also means to loose and to neglect. If you miss one service, you have neglected that one moment of time, so when Hebrews 10:25 says not forsaking, it means not neglecting. We must ask how often we can miss a service before God considers it neglect.   If you do not do something one hundred times, is that neglecting? If you do not do something fifty times, is that neglecting, or if you do not do something ten times, is that neglecting? It will lock you in.

160.   Neglect means that if you do something for one hundred days and you do not do it the one hundred first day, you have neglected it for that day. Hebrews 10:25 does not say not forsaking after the first hundred days;

it simply says not forsaking, so if you miss one service, you have neglected that one day.

161.   Galatians 5:9 says,

9 A little leaven leaveneth the whole lump.

162.   Some believe they do not have to assemble themselves together with the body of Christ because they listen on the Internet or shortwave radio, but Hebrews 10:25 does not say, *"not listening or hearing;"* it says, **"not forsaking the assembling of yourselves together."**

163.   People can hear my message as far away as China and Africa; anyone with a computer can hear me anywhere worldwide. They can hear everything I say, dance to every song, and holler, "Whoop de doo!" when the cheerleaders perform, but they have not assembled with the body of Christ.

164.   When you assemble around the radio or computer, you may be assembling in spirit, but the bible says, **"Not forsaking the assembling of yourselves together."**   Forsaken also means to apostatize; apostatize means abandoning or deserting one's religion, so if you neglect to go to the house of God and assemble, you have deserted God's word.

165.   Strongs' definition of the word "forsaking" is [5]

1459 egkataleipo eng-kat-al-i'-po;

- *from 1722 and 2641; to leave behind in some place, i.e. in a good sense let remain over, or in a bad sense to desert:*

166.   To forsake something means you only do it once; you do not have to do it all the time. I realize it seems as crazy as hell that attending church week after week to hear a man teach is extremely important to God; it seems crazy to me, too, but 1 Corinthians 1:21 says,

21 For after that in the wisdom of God the world by wisdom knew not God, it pleased God by the foolishness of preaching to save them that believe.

167.   Yes, it sounds crazy; some would prefer sitting on the beach today, fulfilling the desires of their stinking flesh, but instead, they are sitting here grasping the words of eternity for eternal life. I also believe you could miss a service without getting behind because I could get you caught up later, but that is not the point. Getting behind or catching up is not the point because God said, *"not forsaking."*

168.   Thayer's definition of the word "forsaking" is
[6]

1459 egkataleipo-

- *to abandon, to desert*
- *to leave in straits, to leave helpless*
- *totally abandoned, utterly forsaken*
- *to leave behind among, to leave surviving*

131

169.   You may argue that you did not abandon God because you only missed one service, but you did abandon that one service.

170.   Strongs' definition of the word "forsaking" is [7]

2641 kataleipo kat-al-i'-po;

- *from 2596 and 3007; to leave down, i.e. behind; by implication, to abandon, have remaining:*

3007 leipo li'-po;

- *a primary verb; to leave, i.e. intransitively or passively to fail or be absent:*

171.   And Thayer's definition of the word "forsaking" is [8]

2641 kataleipo-

- *to leave behind*
- *to depart from, to leave, to be left*
- *to bid one to remain*
- *to forsake, to leave to oneself a person or a thing by ceasing to care for it, to abandon, to leave in the lurch, to be abandoned, to be forsaken*
- *to cause to be left over, to reserve, to leave remaining*

- *like our leave behind, it is used of one who on being called away cannot take another with him*
- *especially of the dying to leave behind*
- *like our leave, leave alone, disregard*
- *of those who sail past a place without stopping*

172.   If you miss one service, you have let down for that one day.

173.   Luke 4:4 says,

4 And Jesus answered him, saying, It is written, That man shall not live by bread alone, but by every word of God.

174.   Forsaking means one who sails past a place without stopping, so when you come upon some of God's words that say, *"not forsaking,"* but you miss a service, you have just sailed past God's word without stopping, and you have forsaken him; it does not matter if you miss one, two or a hundred services.

175.   Again, Galatians 5:9 says,

9 A little leaven leaveneth the whole lump.

176.   If you miss one service, you have sailed by God's word on that day. If you miss one hundred services, you have sailed by God's word a hundred times. The word forsake means to sail without stopping. You did not obey God that day; you just sailed on because you had things to do.

177.   You could not attend church to hear the word taught concerning the precious blood of the Lamb because you had things to do, making the statement that your life is more important to you than hearing the word. It should wake you up because you know that cannot be right. I built this church on the foundational doctrine of *"not forsaking the assembling of yourselves together."*

178.   Hebrews 10:25 of the New International Version says,

25 Let us not give up meeting together, as some are in the habit of doing, but let us encourage one another-- and all the more as you see the Day approaching.

179.   It could mean missing a service or leaving the church altogether, which means you have sailed right on past without stopping; if you have a habit, you must do something more than once, but it does not mean you quit doing it altogether.

180.   When people quit attending church, they do not have a habit, but if they occasionally miss church, they have a habit. We should not be like those with such a habit; instead, we should encourage one another as we see the day approaching.

181.   Hebrews 10:25 of the New American Standard version says,

25 not forsaking our own assembling together, as is the habit of some, but encouraging {one another} and all the more, as you see the day drawing near.

134

182.   And Hebrews 10:25 of the Revised Standard Version says,

25 not neglecting to meet together, as is the habit of some, but encouraging one another, and all the more as you see the Day drawing near.

183.   God is specifically talking to people who do not attend church regularly; they are neglectful. Hebrews 10:25 says that we should not neglect our church meetings. People who occasionally miss a service defend their actions by saying they have not forsaken God.

184.   The Revised Standard Version says, *"not neglecting to meet together,"* so if you miss one service, you have neglected it. In their minds, they have not forsaken God but neglected to come at that moment, which is what forsaking means.

185.   We should gather together in spirit; if you are in China or Russia, you can gather with me in spirit right now. Those who moved here from out of state gathered together in spirit around the radio or computer, but eventually, the message magnetized them to where the body of Christ assembles.

186.   After moving here and committing themselves to attend this church, if they were to miss a service, they would be "neglecting." God gave some out-of-state people a chance to move here, with a way made for them, but they did not come. Only blind people could not see the opportunity God presented to them.

187.	They used the same excuses the people in the Bible used. They just married a wife and cannot come, or they have a career and cannot come. The Bible says that we should not neglect to gather ourselves together.

188.	Again, if an emergency over which you have no control keeps you from attending, your faith counts as if you attended, but if you do not attend church because you have something else to do, you have deliberately planned not to come to that service, which means you neglected that service.

189.	Hebrews 10:26 of the Living Bible says,

26 If anyone sins deliberately by rejecting the Savior after knowing the truth of forgiveness, this sin is not covered by Christ's death; there is no way to get rid of it.

190.	There is no way around this. If you neglect to attend church, even one time, you only have God's anger and a terrible punishment ahead of you. Again, forsaken means neglectful, rejecting, or desertion. God locked you in by two or three things, and you cannot get around it. In the Greek language, the phrase assembling together is one word. When we assemble spiritually, we are in one mind and one place.

Assembling
191.	Acts 2:17 says,

17 And it shall come to pass in the last days, saith God, I will pour out of my Spirit upon all flesh: and your sons and your daughters shall prophesy, and your young men shall see visions, and your old men shall dream dreams:

136

192.   They were in the spirit, in the word, and in the same knowledge together, but also the same building.

193.   1 Corinthians 1:10 says,

10 Now I beseech you, brethren, by the name of our Lord Jesus Christ, that ye all speak the same thing, and that there be no divisions among you; but that ye be perfectly joined together in the same mind and in the same judgment.

194.   And Proverbs 27:17 says,

17 Iron sharpeneth iron; so a man sharpeneth the countenance of his friend.

195.   If you are at home listening to the service, it is different from sitting beside a brother or sister in the church. At home, you can clap your hands, dance to the music, and hear the Word taught, but having a brother or sister sitting beside you is like having a battery charger charging you up.

196.   The Holy Spirit charges you when you and the person beside you look at each other and nod because you are in unity of mind. You are singing and feeling it simultaneously, bringing a supercharge of energy to prepare you for the week.

197.   You are more than a conqueror, an overcomer; standing with someone is much easier than being on an island alone. When you attend church, you experience victory together. I do not know why anyone would not want this.

198.   Strongs' definition of the word "assembling" is
[9]

1997 episunagoge ep-ee-soon-ag-o-gay';

- *from 1996; a complete collection; especially a Christian meeting for worship:*

199.   You cannot do this spiritually; you can collect your minds together spiritually, but Christians must assemble their physical bodies together for worship.

200.   Thayer's definition of the word "assembling" is [10]

1997 episunagoge-

- *a gathering together in one place*
- *the religious assembly of Christians*

201.   Some believe that "one place" is in the word. I do, as well. I preach that doctrine very strongly; I am the one who fathered the modern-day teaching that the word is spirit and life. I believe we gather together in spirit, mind, hope, and faith, but that starts with us gathering ourselves together in one place for a religious assembly.

202.   I am not knocking radio, the Internet, and recordings; I praise God for them, but I am telling you that these media are just nets. You can only build your faith to a certain level while on a line, hook, or in a net. You must allow the man of God to draw you into the boat.

203.   When Noah preached that it would rain, his message was the net, and those who got on the ark were in the net; it meant a gathering in one place. People who got on the ark were together in mind because they had to believe the same thing to get on it. Also, they gathered together in spirit because the leading of God brought them to the ark; they gathered together in unity on the ark, where they physically gathered together.

204.   What would have happened if people had told Noah that they would not get on the ark but were still with him spiritually? They would have drowned just like those who did not respond to or believe in his message. Many rejected that one small point of physically coming together and drowned.

205.   If you physically come together but do not come together in spirit and mind, you damn yourself; you must have it all and come together physically, mentally, spiritually, and with unity in the word.

206.   Again, 1 Corinthians 1:10 says,

10 Now I beseech you, brethren, by the name of our Lord Jesus Christ, that ye all speak the same thing, and that there be no divisions among you; but that ye be perfectly joined together in the same mind and in the same judgment.

207.   Think about those who told Noah they were with him in spirit but would not get on the ark with him. I would tell you to keep your dirty spirit away from here if you do not obey God's word. I do not say that to everyone because some may still need a chance to get hooked, but once the hook secures itself and they

do not obey God's word, I will say it to them. I hooked some who are here and others who are not here. Those not here, God has cursed with a curse and damned them.

208.   Hebrews 3:15 says,

15 While it is said, To day if ye will hear his voice, harden not your hearts, as in the provocation.

209.   What if some of the apostles told Peter they were not going to the upper room with him but would be there in spirit? The only ones who received the Holy Ghost were those physically in the upper room.

210.   Again, Proverbs 27:17 says,

17 Iron sharpeneth iron; so a man sharpeneth the countenance of his friend.

211.   There is more power in numbers.

212.   Matthew 18:20 says,

20 For where two or three are gathered together in my name, there am I in the midst of them.

213.   When we gather together, more than three people are present, allowing us to sharpen and make each other worship more intensely.

214.   Strongs' further definition of the word "assembling" is [11]

- *episunago ep-ee-soon-ag'-o;*

- *from 1909 and 4863; to collect upon the same place:*

215.   It means you must come together spiritually, mentally, and physically.

216.   Thayer's further definition of the word "assembling" is [12]

1996 episunago-

- *to gather together beside, to bring together to others who are already assembled*
- *to gather together against*
- *to gather together in one place*

217.   We must assemble.

218.   Strongs' further definition of the word "assembling" is [13]

4863 sunago soon-ag'-o;

- *from 4862 and 71; to lead together, i.e. collect or convene; specifically, to entertain hospitably:*

- *accompany, assemble selves, together, bestow, come together, gather selves together, up, together, lead into, resort, take in.*

219.   We convene here every Sunday, which is what assembling means; when the Bible says to assemble ourselves, it is not talking abstractly.   It means we

141

should not forsake coming together. If you listen at home, you know things around your house will distract you, but if you remove yourself from that setting and place yourself in an environment without distractions, you can concentrate better. Therefore, you will have a different perspective of the message than if you had listened to it alone.

220.   Concerning the definition of the word forsaken, I have proven that it means to miss only one time because assembling does not mean just in the spirit; it means to convene in a place, so we are all bound to it.

221.   Again, Hebrews 10:25 says,

25 Not forsaking the assembling of ourselves together, as the manner of some is; but exhorting one another: and so much the more, as ye see the day approaching.

222.   Strongs' definition of the word "more" is [14]

3123 mallon mal'-lon;

- *neuter of the comparative of the same as 3122; adverbially more in a greater degree or rather:*

- *better, X far, the more and more, so much the more, rather.*

223.   You should attend church more often, but more importantly, when you attend church, you should go with more intent each time.

224.   Thayer's definition of the word "more" is [15]

- *more, to a greater degree; rather*

- *increase, a greater quantity, a larger measure, a higher degree, more, more fully*

- *much, by far, Mark 10:48*

- *in comparison it often so stands that than before must be mentally added A.V., the more, so much the more, as Matt 27:24*

- *what moreover is of greater moment A.V., yea rather: Rom 8:34*

- *it marks the preference of one thing above another, and is to be rendered rather, sooner*

- *it denotes that which occurs more easily than something else, and may be rendered sooner Matt 6:30*
- *the rather*

- *after a preceding negative or prohibitive sentence: Matt 10:6,28*

- *so that mallon belongs to the thing which is preferred, consequently to a noun, not to a verb: John 3:19*

- *by way of correction, mallon de, nay rather; to speak more correctly: Gal 4:9*

143

- *it does not do away with that with which it is in opposition, but marks what has the preference: more willingly, more readily, sooner*

225.   It means that when we see the day approaching or believe the end of time is coming, we should increase our efforts in assembling together, talking with each other, fellowshipping with each other, and hearing the word of God to a greater degree because it preferences one thing more important than another.

226.   "More" does not do away with what is in its opposition; instead, it marks what has the preference. It is the key definition. The word more denotes what has a preference. Some want me to cut down on how many services we have. That shows their preferences.

227.   If you prefer worshipping God, you should want me to have more services because that is the faith-filling station. We carry God with us everywhere we go, but his presence rests here and sets here at the church building. He waits for our return so that he can move among us. Outside of church, we are witnesses, but in church, it is just God and us. Why would anyone not want to be a part of that?

228.   He said, **"Not forsaking the assembling of yourselves together above all as you see the day approaching."** He means, above all, which locks us in. The phrase *"The much more"* means above all your life, circumstances, job, house, family, and reasons; it should be above everything else in your life.

229.   Everything else comes second, including your job; if you put your job before God during the

144

appointed times for assembling yourself together, causing you to neglect a service or two every week, you should change jobs.

230.   The phrase *"so the much more"* means above all and not forsaking, so if you attend the house of God, I can pound faith into you; even if you are hard-headed and a fool, I can find the key to your success and brain.

231.   If you are home, you can get up and cook a steak, have a beer, and flush the toilet a few times while I preach, but if you attend church, I can get in your mind, so "*not forsaking the assembling of yourselves together*" means you should not miss church or quit altogether.

232.   If you quit, Hebrews 6:4 says that it is impossible for God to renew you. I hope you get the whole picture. Hebrews 10:25-26 is not talking about quitting church altogether; it says that if you occasionally neglect to come, there is no more sacrifice for sin - Hebrews 6:4 talks about quitting church altogether, so based on these scriptures, God will not save you if you quit church, or miss a service.

233.   If you quit or miss a service, you believe your will is more important than God's. We may be the only church worldwide that preaches this doctrine; other ministers say they cannot enforce it because if they do not allow those who missed church to return, everyone will eventually leave.

234.   These ministers want a big crowd so they do not have to work a regular job. If they continually put people out, they would not make enough money to

support themselves and would eventually have to get regular jobs.

235.   I prefer to work a regular job because I can forget it once I go home; it is just a job. I would rather be poor than have to take my job home with me. When I get home, I want to forget the damn job, so I prefer a regular job where I can do the same thing every day and not have to think about it when I get home.

236.   These ministers are so adamant about not wanting to work a regular job that they are willing to keep rebellious people in their congregation. When people miss a service in my ministry, I will not let them back anymore.

237.   Again, Hebrews 10:25 says,

25 Not forsaking the assembling of ourselves together, as the manner of some is; but exhorting one another: and so much the more, as ye see the day approaching.

238.   We should not neglect to assemble ourselves together with our minds, spirits, and bodies, but most importantly, we must physically assemble ourselves together. I know how to get around the scripture that says we should not commit adultery because all you need is grace through faith, but I do not know how to get around the following scripture.

239.   Matthew 6:34 says,

34 Take therefore no thought for the morrow: for the morrow shall take thought for the things of itself. Sufficient unto the day is the evil thereof.

240.   God gives us just enough faith and grace for each day. You must be where the man of God is dispensing faith so you will have the grace to cover you for your daily living. If you are unwilling to go where the dunamis fires, you neglect the assembling, will not receive grace, and will frustrate it.

241.   Grace does not cover missing church because attending church is how you get faith. Faith is what ignites grace. You go to church to get faith because faith makes grace work. Many say they love God, even though they do not attend every service. They do not believe God will be angry with them and believe they can miss church and still love God, but 1 John 2:4 says,

4 He that saith, I know him, and keepeth not his commandments, is a liar, and the truth is not in him.

242.   God's commandment says, *"not forsaking the assembling of ourselves together,"* so if you intentionally miss a service but still claim that you love God, 1 John 2:4 says you are a liar. God is always right. If he says you are a liar, but you claim you are not, I will believe God.

243.   Some claim that God is first in their lives and that we are at the end of time; they believe I am preaching the truth, but they do not want to attend church tonight. There is something more important they want to do, at least at that moment, than attending the house of God, so it became first with them on that day.

244.   If it was first with them on that day, it is also on other days. Of course, it was more convenient for

them to attend church the next time, but when the next inconvenient time comes, they will miss it again; there must be a sacrifice.

245.   The church is here for God's pleasure and convenience, not yours; the church world has done it to you again by raping your mind and causing you to think that the church is about you, for you, and here to lift you. Wrong! The church is about God, and assembling is about pleasing God! In return, he gives us faith.

246.   1 John 2:4 of the New American Standard version of the Bible says,

4 The one who says, I have come to know Him, and does not keep His commandments, is a liar, and the truth is not in him;

247.   And 1 John 2:4 of the New International Version says,

4 The man who says, I know him, but does not do what he commands is a liar, and the truth is not in him.

248.   And 1 John 2:4 of the New King James Version says,

4 He who says, I know Him, and does not keep His commandments, is a liar, and the truth is not in him.

249.   And 1 John 2:4 of the Revised Standard Version says,

4 He who says I know him but disobeys his commandments is a liar, and the truth is not in him;

250.   And 1 John 2:4 of The Living Bible says,

4 Someone may say, I am a Christian; I am on my way to heaven; I belong to Christ. But if he doesn't do what Christ tells him to, he is a liar.

251.   And 1 John 2:4 of the American Standard Version says,

4 He that saith, I know him, and keepeth not his commandments, is a liar, and the truth is not in him;

252.   Finally, Luke 4:4 of the King James Version says,

4 And Jesus answered him, saying, It is written, That man shall not live by bread alone, but by every word of God.

253.   Hebrews 10:25 is a part of the word of God.

254.   1 John 4:20 says,

20 If a man say, I love God, and hateth his brother, he is a liar: for he that loveth not his brother whom he hath seen, how can he love God whom he hath not seen?

255.   And John 14:15 says,

15 If ye love me, keep my commandments.

256.   Some do not believe that Hebrews 10:25 is God's commandment.

If You Love Jesus
257.   John 14:23 says,

23 Jesus answered and said unto him, If a man love me, he will keep my words: and my Father will love him, and we will come unto him, and make our abode with him.

258.   If you miss church, you are a liar; God is not abiding in you, nor is he with you. You damn yourself and go to hell because you neglected the Holy One. You forsook God, at least for that moment, and you showed him that there was something in your life more important on that day than him.

259.   It could be your spouse, your anniversary, or your reunion. You may not like me and think I am too hard, but when you are in trouble and want a real preacher, one you know is not playing, you will call me (the one you do not like). You know that if I did not mean it, I would not say it. I could have a larger congregation if I did not preach these messages.

260.   There is a story about a soldier on the battlefield. There was a fierce battle raging, and many soldiers died. Simultaneously, the enemy shot two soldiers. They fell on the battlefield. One soldier was Protestant, and the other was Catholic.

261.   A minister went to the Protestant soldier and prayed over him because he would die. As he prayed, the Catholic soldier saw him and noticed that he prayed

directly to Jesus. When a Catholic priest came to him, he told the Catholic soldier to join him as he prayed to Mary.

262.   The Catholic soldier told him, "No, I want that minister to pray for me." The Catholic priest asked him why he wanted a Protestant minister to pray for him since he was Catholic. The Catholic soldier replied, "I am dying, so I do not want to go through any secretaries; I want to go to the main guy."

263.   Similarly, they may say I am wrong and do not believe what I preach, but when they get into trouble and need a man of God, they call me because they know I am not playing; I call it as it is. Everyone knows that if I allowed people to attend church when they wanted, some would only attend occasionally. They play with God, and I will not let anyone play in my ministry.

264.   John 15:10 says,

10 If ye keep my commandments, ye shall abide in my love; even as I have kept my Father's commandments, and abide in his love.

265.   And John 15:10 of the New American Standard Bible says,

10 If you keep My commandments, you will abide in My love; just as I have kept My Father's commandments, and abide in His love.

266.   And John 15:10 of the New International Version says,

10 If you obey my commands, you will remain in my love, just as I have obeyed my Father's commands and remain in his love.

267.   And John 15:10 of the New King James Version says,

10 If you keep My commandments, you will abide in My love, just as I have kept My Father's commandments and abide in His love.

268.   And John 15:10 of the Revised Standard Version says,

10 If you keep my commandments, you will abide in my love, just as I have kept my Father's commandments and abide in his love.

269.   And John 15:10 of The Living Bible says,

10 When you obey me you are living in my love, just as I obey my Father and live in his love.

270.   Finally, John 15:10 of the American Standard Version says,

10 If ye keep my commandments, ye shall abide in my love; even as I have kept my Father's commandments, and abide in his love.

271.   John 8:31 says,

31 Then said Jesus to those Jews which believed on him, If ye continue in my word, then are ye my disciples indeed;

272.   And John 8:31 of the New American Standard Bible says,

31 Jesus therefore was saying to those Jews who had believed Him, If you abide in My word, {then} you are truly disciples of Mine;

273.   And John 8:31 of the New International Version says,

31 To the Jews who had believed him, Jesus said, If you hold to my teaching, you are really my disciples.

274.   And John 8:31 of the New King James Version says,

31 Then Jesus said to those Jews who believed Him, If you abide in My word, you are My disciples indeed.

275.   And John 8:31 of the Revised Standard Version says,

31 Jesus then said to the Jews who had believed in him, If you continue in my word, you are truly my disciples,

276.   And John 8:31 of the Living Bible says,

31 Then many of the Jewish leaders who heard him say these things began believing him to be the Messiah. Jesus said to them, You are truly my disciples if you live as I tell you to,

277.   And John 8:31 of the American Standard Version says,

153

31 Jesus therefore said to those Jews that had believed him, If ye abide in my word, then are ye truly my disciples;

278. Strongs' definition of the word "continue" is
[16]

3306 meno men'-o;

- *a primary verb; to stay in a given place, state, relation or expectancy:*

- <u>*abide*</u>*, continue, dwell, endure, be present, remain, stand, tarry for, X thine own.*

279. You are not his disciples if you do not abide in his word, so if you do not believe and practice Hebrews 10:25, you are not a child of God. It does not matter if you speak in tongues until you are blue in the face. Why? Because you broke his word.

280. Again, 1 Samuel 15:22 says,

22 And Samuel said, Hath the LORD as great delight in burnt offerings and sacrifices, as in obeying the voice of the LORD? Behold, to obey is better than sacrifice, and to hearken than the fat of rams.

281. Hebrews 13:17 says,

17 Obey them that have the rule over you, and submit yourselves: for they watch for your souls, as they that must give account, that they may do it with joy, and not with grief: for that is unprofitable for you.

282.   And Matthew 6:21 says,

21 For where your treasure is, there will your heart be also.

283.   If you are more excited about picking up a new car than attending the house of God, your treasure is in that car, not God.

284.   Finally, Isaiah 26:3 says,

3 Thou wilt keep him in perfect peace, whose mind is stayed on thee: because he trusteth in thee.

References

1. PCStudy Bible, Electronic Database. 1996 Biblesoft

2. Ibid.

3. Ibid.

4. Roget's New Millennium™ Thesaurus, First Edition v 1.3.1, Copyright © 2007, by Lexico Publishing Group, LLC. www.dictionary.com

5. PCStudy Bible, Electronic Database. 1996 Biblesoft

6. Ibid.

7. Ibid.

8. Ibid.

9. Ibid.

10. Ibid.

11. Ibid.

12. Ibid.

13. Ibid.

14. Ibid.

15. From Thayer's Greek Lexicon, Electronic Database. Copyright © 2000 by Biblesoft

16. PCStudy Bible, Electronic Database. 1996 Biblesoft

Chapter Four
The Assembling Covenant

1. If you read the New Testament, you will discover that every spiritual experience occurred when the body of Christ gathered together, so Paul had a right to require his congregation to gather because God established it in the Old Testament.

2. Genesis 3:7 says,

7 And the eyes of them both were opened, and they knew that they were naked; and they sewed fig leaves together, and made themselves aprons.

3. Adam and Eve walked the earth for an unknown amount of time before they fell; they did it naked without knowing it. I am unsure why they did not know because all the animals were naked, but God did not want people to have mirrors, so they never saw themselves. Perhaps they knew they did not have clothes, but not that God considered it naked because he had not revealed sin to them. After they ate, their eyes opened, and they knew they were naked.

4. Genesis 3:8-10 says,

8 And they heard the voice of the Lord God walking in the garden in the cool of the day: and Adam and his wife hid themselves from the presence of the Lord God amongst the trees of the garden.

9 And the Lord God called unto Adam, and said unto him, Where art thou?

10 And he said, I heard thy voice in the garden, and I was afraid, because I was naked; and I hid myself.

5.   Have you heard that voice? Today, if you hear his voice (Hebrews 3:15). I heard the voice in the garden, a place of great delight or peace. Adam was afraid because he was naked, so he heard the voice. He did his fleshly work by trying to hide through his rule of sewing fig leaves, which is where the damnable doctrine of let us cover ourselves came in.

6.   Before that, God's grace covered them. It occurred prior to the law when they were under grace. Many Christians try to hide their sins, but they are wretches behind walls of rules (thou shalt, and thou shalt not). That is where it started. First, Eve is responsible, and then it falls to Adam because he went along with it.

7.   Genesis 3:11 says,

11 And he said, Who told thee that thou wast naked? Hast thou eaten of the tree, whereof I commanded thee that thou shouldest not eat?

8.   I would have asked them if they had listened to another preacher. God was more concerned about who told him they were naked than their nakedness. God does not like gossip.

9.   Genesis 3:12-13 says,

12 And the man said, The woman whom thou gavest to be with me, she gave me of the tree, and I did eat.

13 And the Lord God said unto the woman, What is this that thou hast done? And the woman said, The serpent beguiled me, and I did eat.

10. In the New Testament, Jesus called false preachers serpents. Beguiled means to be sexually seduced. It is essential to notice that God is angrier at those who told. He is not angry at Adam and Eve's nakedness; he is mad because they listened to another preacher. In Genesis 3:14-15 God curses the serpent.

11. Genesis 3:16-17 says,

16 Unto the woman he said, I will greatly multiply thy sorrow and thy conception; in sorrow thou shalt bring forth children; and thy desire shall be to thy husband, and he shall rule over thee.

17 And unto Adam he said, Because thou hast hearkened unto the voice of thy wife, and hast eaten of the tree, of which I commanded thee, saying, Thou shalt not eat of it: cursed is the ground for thy sake; in sorrow shalt thou eat of it all the days of thy life;

The Voice of the Lord
12. Men must rule their wives; if not, they are out of order. You rule through leadership and, if necessary, metaphorically bring the rod of iron down. If you are afraid to lose your woman, you are in a relationship of fear, not love.

13. God cursed Adam because he hearkened to the voice of his wife. The woman made him do something that kept him out of church that day. It is difficult for me to believe that this is the first time in history that

the voice of the Lord walked in the garden, and Adam and Eve happened to know it. There had to be other times because they knew where it was, and when they heard him, they hid among the trees.

14. It tells me that they knew where the voice came to walk and speak because they heard him walking in the garden. How would they hear him if they did not know the location? Adam and the voice of the Lord had likely been regularly communing because God wanted to commune with someone, and he had great confidence in Adam; even if they had never met or spoken before (I believe they did), they had an appointment that day.

15. The voice of the Lord walked in the garden and knew the location; Adam and Eve did, too. God agreed with Adam to meet at a specific place and time. If you have a friend, your conversation has been continuous since you first met, just as God's word continues.

16. If you disagree because I do not have a direct scripture that proves my point, I can still say that even if it was the first day, they knew the location and time of where and when they were to meet, but on this day, they decided not to attend the gathering.

17. In Matthew 18:20, Jesus said,

20 For where two or three are gathered together in my name, there am I in the midst of them.

18. This story is the foundation for the prior verse because the voice of the Lord, Adam and Eve, would have been in attendance. It established that we must

assemble ourselves. The voice of the Lord asked where they were; he expected their presence. There was a location called the Cool of the Day, and they should have been there.

19. However, Eve heard another gospel and brought it home to Adam, making it her fault that they missed the church service that day. Adam decided not to go because he knew they were naked, making him responsible at that point; they should have attended. Although Eve kept them from church that day because of what she did, it should not have, but they thought it did.

20. For example, if someone takes a weekend off to attend an anniversary party, they do not think they forsook and broke away because it was a momentary thing. That is what they thought, too, but they should have attended church naked because they should have sought the kingdom of God first.

21. Since Adam heard the voice of the Lord walking, not talking, he was close to the location or meeting place. If this meeting were not preplanned, there would be no reason for the voice of the Lord to ask for Adam.

22. They decided to miss one service because they did not have the right kind of clothes. I wonder what message they would have heard that day. Undoubtedly, they had heard many others because the voice of the Lord expected them to be there.

23. Since they missed church and listened to a false gospel once, God cursed everyone. Had they attended

that day, we could have avoided all the hell we must live in, including getting up early to work. Nevertheless, the voice of the Lord was angry because they were not at the assembly place; Eve went to another's gathering; she and the serpent had a religious exchange. They talked about what God had said.

Participating in False Religion
24. Ephesians 5:11 says,

11 And have no fellowship with the unfruitful works of darkness, but rather reprove them.

25. She returned to Adam, and he participated in false religious activity. This story encompasses all evil. Eve received that information by fellowshipping someone who talked about what God said. She may have thought, "What can go wrong? We are talking about God." A lot can go wrong if you have listened to the voice of the Lord but later hear some other voice or minister.

26. John 10:4-5 says,

4 And when he putteth forth his own sheep, he goeth before them, and the sheep follow him: for they know his voice.

5 And a stranger will they not follow, but will flee from him: for they know not the voice of strangers.

27. Therefore, God established assembling together to hear the voice of the Lord in the third chapter of Genesis when he said, "Where art thou?" To our

knowledge, they only missed one service; it agrees with Hebrews 10:25-26, which says,

25 Not forsaking the assembling of ourselves together, as the manner of some is; but exhorting one another: and so much the more, as ye see the day approaching.

26 For if we sin wilfully after that we have received the knowledge of the truth, there remaineth no more sacrifice for sins,

28. The first church service a child of God missed was in Genesis 3 when church services began. They probably did not have a building, but they had a meeting place, a gathering place.

29. Matthew 24:28 says,

28 For wheresoever the carcase is, there will the eagles be gathered together.

30. Watching television or listening to the radio program is not gathering together, but someone may say, "It does mean in spirit." In the Bible, when they gathered together in spirit, they also did it physically because one can put a thousand to flight and two can put ten thousand to flight (Deuteronomy 32:30).

31. When the entire body comes together in one place, it is together as one, but you miss it if you are not there. If you get a recording, you will miss what God did at that moment because his work is in the hearts of men, and you cannot write it or record it.

32. If you were here, heard a sermon, and later listened to the recording, you can get more from it, but if you were not here, you would only get what is on the recording because you missed the service, the anointing, and God's presence for that time. That is what Adam and Eve did, so those who think it is permissible to miss even one service should stop lying to themselves because anyone who denies Hebrews 10:25 is not Christian.

33. Matthew 6:33 says,

33 But seek ye first the kingdom of God, and his righteousness; and all these things shall be added unto you.

Missing Church

34. If you miss church for any reason, it becomes more important than the service you know would occur years in advance. At that moment, whatever you did other than attend church becomes more important to you than God's word, and you are accountable. It is not just about hearing the message; it also includes gathering together.

35. You must remember that God is jealous, selfish, and picky, so you better be there if he wants your carcass in the church to hear his voice! If God sends his voice and you ignore it to do anything but listen to it, you have disrespected God, and he will not forgive you. Some of these same people will judge others for what they wear while they break the primary covenant.

36. Some hesitate to attend other churches because they do not believe their preacher is a true man of God;

164

if so, you should do what Revelation 18:4 says and come out! Find the voice walking in the garden; it will not always sound sweet, kind, or loving, but it will fight for you!

37. The same voice that searched for Adam and Eve is speaking tonight; it has been speaking to this congregation for a long time. I believe the voice of the Lord would have given Adam and Eve a revelation they had not heard before, but they did not attend church that day.

38. Every preacher ought to love this book because it will instruct their congregations to attend without missing, but they will not like it because half the church will leave if the ministers enforce it. If so, they have already left and are damned.

39. If a minister does not enforce this doctrine for fear of losing your church you are doing what Adam did by hearkening to his wife's voice; you are hearkening to the voice of your congregation. Some preachers have wives who get mad at them if they do not take them on vacations, even if it interferes with planned gatherings. You should get rid of the cow and put God first!

Be Ye Perfect
40. Matthew 5:48 says,

48 Be ye therefore perfect, even as your Father which is in heaven is perfect.

41. That is a command, not a suggestion. God did not say we should do our best; he commanded us to be perfect. Those who live by rules cannot honestly say

they are perfect in the flesh, so they fail this commandment. We must be as perfect as God, which sets the bar very high.

42. You have failed if you try to be as perfect as humanly possible. We might have the willpower to live like another human, but we cannot live perfectly like God. Matthew 5:48 condemns everyone who does not believe and practices the message of grace the way Paul and I preach it. God does not fail in perfection or sin or make errors.

43. Matthew 5:48 (The Living Bible) says,

48 But you are to be perfect, even as your Father in heaven is perfect.

44. Matthew 5:48 (Amplified Bible) says,

48 You, therefore, must be perfect [growing into complete maturity of godliness in mind and character, having reached the proper height of virtue and integrity], as your heavenly Father is perfect.

45. We must be like God, so there is no variableness, neither shadow of turning (James 1:17).

46. Leviticus 19:2 says,

2 Speak unto all the congregation of the children of Israel, and say unto them, Ye shall be holy: for I the Lord your God am holy.

47. We must be perfect and holy like God. What can a human possibly do to be as perfect as God on Earth?

Some may say, "He gives us the Holy Ghost to keep us pure." You cannot find one person in the Bible who received the Holy Ghost that was sinless or without mistakes. God gave the Holy Ghost to lead and guide us into all truth.

Ministers Must Not Forsake
48. God's word is not only for the sheep to obey, but ministers must also obey it. I should not preach the word to the sheep while living another life. Jesus was the example, and I must follow him as a minister.

49. Paul said in 1 Corinthians 11:1,

1 Be ye followers of me, even as I also am of Christ.

50. Jesus said in John 13:15,

15 For I have given you an example, that ye should do as I have done to you.

51. Jesus did not break the word of God, ignore it, make it second in his life, or put it behind all his needs and wants. Some ministers preach Hebrews 10:25-26 to their congregation but do not obey it themselves.

52. Hebrews 10:25-26 says,

25 Not forsaking the assembling of ourselves together, as the manner of some is; but exhorting one another: <u>and so much the more</u>, as ye see the day approaching.

26 For if we sin wilfully after that we have received the knowledge of the truth, there remaineth no more sacrifice for sins,

53. During the crucifixion, Jesus was under stress and injured. During his trial, he was up all night and all day with no sleep, no rest, and no food, and then they took him straight to the cross. Before these events, he prayed in Gethsemane, "Lord, if it be thou will let this cup pass from me," his sweat became great drops of blood because of the stress.

54. If anybody could have used a vacation away from it all to clear their mind and enjoy and fulfill their wife's desires, it would have been Jesus. He could have left and gone to Greece, Italy, or the French Riviera, but he stayed to fulfill God's will. He did not take a break for us. While on the cross, Jesus thirsted because he had nothing to eat or drink since the previous day. Jesus was so weak that he could not carry his cross; someone else had to carry it.

55. They crucified him between 9 a.m. and 12 p.m., and he died between 12 p.m. and 3 p.m. during a great eclipse, so he definitely could have used a break that day, but he did not take one because of us. God turned away from him, and Jesus took the entire weight of our sins upon him. He died a horrible death for us and could have used a vacation then, but he stayed the course as our example.

56. Some ministers have the gall to preach Hebrews 10:25-26 to their congregation, saying they must be in church, but when their wives want to take a vacation or their family wants to do something, or when the minister wants to go somewhere, they will miss church in a second while telling the congregation not to miss.

57. I recently heard a minister tell his congregation that he would miss church for two Sundays but told his people not to miss it because they should continue to attend without a break. I spoke to this preacher and said, "I wish you would rethink this Greece trip." I did not tell him why. I told him I get my vacation by visiting my studio or church and hanging out there. Also, church time is my vacation.

58. He replied, "I feel the same way. I do not care about going to Greece. I do not care about going anywhere; I enjoy my vacation at the church, but my wife does not feel the same way, so I must go because she wants to go."

59. If it were me, I would tell the wife to go to hell; I would stay and obey God's word! Until about ten years ago, I never took a vacation. Every trip I ever took had to do with the ministry. The last couple of years, we went to Western Maryland and hung out with the body of Christ, but we were back here on Friday for church.

60. This congregation is a witness before Almighty God, showing people you can do it correctly because they might say, "Your people never take a vacation." Yes, we do, but we plan our vacations around church services. We even try to plan our death around church services; we try to plan our life around church services.

61. Another minister from Philadelphia taught Hebrews 10:25 but countered it by saying, "If you have to work on Tuesday night, you are not breaking the scripture by staying out of the church to go to work because the Bible says if you do not work, you do not

eat." I agree, but the Bible did not say you had to work a job that kept you from attending church.

62. Matthew 6:33 says,

33 But seek ye first the kingdom of God, and his righteousness; and all these things shall be added unto you.

Ministers Must Obey God's Word Too

63. If you put God first and avoid taking vacations that interfere with church services at God's appointed time, you will have the most fantastic vacation the world has ever seen, but if you break God's word to have a vacation here on Earth, you will burn in the Lake of Fire, especially ministers who tell their congregation they must attend while they leave for a two-week vacation.

64. My congregation sees me practice everything I preach. I do not cut corners for my earthly family or myself. Some ministers are so scared of demon spirits - what do you think will happen to the flock while you are in Greece because Eve (your wife) wanted to go? Of course, you blamed it on Eve (your wife), but maybe you want to go. You may say, "We have not had a vacation in years." Jesus did not have one, either.

65. Hebrews 12:4 says,

4 Ye have not yet resisted unto blood, striving against sin.

66. What is wrong with you? God gives you breath to breathe, a way to make a living, and supplies your

needs. You may say, "The heathen has these things too." The difference is that Christians give God credit and acknowledge him; the heathen do not.

67. What can you do in life that is more instructive and more upbuilding for the Kingdom of God and your spiritual life outside of attending church? No vacation will do it. However, it is permissible to take a vacation as long as you are on time for church.

68. Ministers should not lay out a church every week, just like the congregation. The only difference is if God tells him to preach somewhere else. That is not missing, but it is hypocritical for a minister to take a vacation that God has not ordained while preaching to his congregation that they should not miss church services. I would not follow that kind of minister; come out of her!

69. If I were as scared and worried about evil spirits as some ministers claim, I would not leave for two weeks. Instead, I would stand with a big sword to defend the church, but some ministers will take a vacation saying, "I can leave an assistant pastor to teach while I am gone."

70. I have heard him preach; God has not called him to teach. He held an Easter play recently while the leading minister allowed it to happen. He said, "I had nothing to do with it; I just sat and watched."

71. No, you are responsible! These Deliverance ministries cast out the same evil spirit weekly. Although it keeps your ministry going, you are a joke, so I understand why you are leaving for vacation.

171

72. However, for those who hear the truth, we look forward to attending church; it ensures we can go on a vacation during the week but return on time for the church service because we want to hear the truth of God's word. The truth includes Hebrews 10:25-26, not forsaking the assembling of ourselves together.

73. Hebrews 10:25-26 says,

25 Not forsaking the assembling of ourselves together, as the manner of some is; but exhorting one another: <u>and so much the more</u>, as ye see the day approaching.

26 For if we sin wilfully after that we have received the knowledge of the truth, there remaineth no more sacrifice for sins,

74. "So much the more;" you should not plan more vacations; you should plan more worship services. Ministers have blessings and freedom that the body of Christ does not have. When God speaks to me, I am hearing in the first person. When I speak to you, you hear in the second person, but as soon as you can stop seeing my flesh and hear, you will hear in the first person. Nevertheless, ministers should obey God's word, too.

75. Again, Jesus said in John 13:15,

15 For I have given you an example, that ye should do as I have done to you.

76. And Luke 9:57-60 says,

57 And it came to pass, that, as they went in the way, a certain man said unto him, Lord, I will follow thee whithersoever thou goest.

58 And Jesus said unto him, Foxes have holes, and birds of the air have nests; but the Son of man hath not where to lay his head.

59 And he said unto another, Follow me. But he said, Lord, suffer me first to go and bury my father.

60 Jesus said unto him, Let the dead bury their dead: but go thou and preach the kingdom of God.

77. Jesus did not believe in missing church for anything; he even told the man to miss his dad's funeral.

78. Hebrews 3:15 says,

15 While it is said, To day if ye will hear his voice, harden not your hearts, as in the provocation.

Forsake Meanings

79. If he heard enough to know that Jesus was the Messiah, Jesus expected him to follow immediately. I spoke to a minister who said, "Just because you miss a service or two here and there does not mean you forsook because 'forsake' means to quit permanently." Of course, if you stop attending church, you have forsaken it, but forsake also has other meanings.

80. Strongs' definition of the word "forsaking" is [1]

5805 `azuwbah az-oo-baw';

173

feminine passive participle of 5800; <u>*desertion*</u>
of inhabitants:

81. You can desert something for a few minutes.

82. Brown-Driver-Brigg's definition of the word
"forsaken" is [2]

> *5800 `azab-*
>
> *to leave, to loose, to forsake*
> *Qal to leave*
> *to depart from, to leave behind, to leave, to let*
> *alone*
> *to leave, to* <u>*abandon*</u>*, to forsake,* <u>*to neglect*</u>*, to*
> *apostatize*
> *to let loose, to set free, to let go, to free*
> *Niphal*
> *to be left to*
> *to be forsaken*
> *Pual to be deserted*
> *to restore, to repair Qal*

83. Neglect means - failing to care for properly, so if
you neglect something, you are not taking it seriously.

84. According to Roget's New Millennium™
Thesaurus, First Edition v 1.3.1 [3]

A synonym for the word "abandon" is <u>*interrupt*</u>*.*

85. Interrupt means - stopping the continuous progress
of (an activity or process). For example, if you are
watching a show, commercials will interrupt it. It does
not go away completely; the commercial has just

174

stopped the continuing progress of the broadcast. After the show returns, you can enjoy it again. In comparison, if you interrupt assembling yourself together, you have not stopped it altogether; you only paused attendance, which means you forsook it.

86. Strongs' definition of the word "forsaking" is [4]

2641 kataleipo kat-al-i'-po;

from 2596 and 3007; to leave down, i.e. behind; by implication, to abandon, have remaining:

3007 leipo li'-po;

a primary verb; to leave, i.e. intransitively or passively to fail or <u>be absent</u>:

87. You can attend church and be absent simultaneously, but you should bring your body to the assembling place; if you go on vacation for a couple of weeks, you are absent, which means you forsook it.

88. Some forsake synonyms are abandon, cut, discontinue, give up, interrupt, <u>pause</u>, rest, and suspend. If you watch a movie on television, you will use the remote control to pause it while going to the bathroom or getting something to eat; you did not abandon it altogether, only for a moment, but you still forsook it.

89. More forsake synonyms are abandon, cancel, clear out, cover, cross out, digress, evade, leave, <u>miss</u>, nullify, omit, overshoot, pass over, skip, and switch. Forsake can mean permanent but also to pause or miss.

175

90. Some will say, "I am not quitting church; I am only taking a vacation." You are pausing, forcing God, his Kingdom, and the heavenly hosts to wait until you return before he can address the entire church. While you are away, a supposed part of the body of Christ is missing; I wonder what they will cause us to miss.

Forsaking Your Relationship

91. If you believe that "forsake" means you quit altogether, but it does not mean to interrupt to pause, to miss, to be absent, and that missing for a couple of weeks or missing a service here or there is not the same thing as forsaking – would you apply that same principle to your relationship?

92. Many use the excuse that "forsake" means leave and not return so they can miss sporadically and believe they have not forsaken. However, the definition says to interrupt or to pause! Would you apply the same definition and scenario to your relationship that you are applying to God?

93. Set aside any agreement you may have beforehand; you are just a couple in love. Say you have been a couple for fifteen years, have done everything together, and have been faithful. Then, one day after work, one of you does not return home at the usual time and arrives eight hours late without calling or making any other contact.

94. After years of being faithful, he or she comes home later than usual and says, "I stopped off with a friend at the bar. We got a drink, left, got a hotel room, and had a couple of hours of sex. I enjoyed my time away from the routine but did not forsake our relationship

176

because I am here now. See, I am here, so I did not leave permanently. I just took a break from us and enjoyed the moment, so I did not forsake it."

95. If you are in a committed relationship and your partner takes a break to cheat and have sex with someone else – would you say that they forsook the relationship by going to a bar and having sex with another person? Would you say that they forsook the relationship at that moment? Even though they are with you now, they forsook the relationship in a way they cannot fully repair. In comparison, that is what you tell God, "Now, Lord, I am going on vacation, but I will return."

96. Exodus 20:3 says,

3 Thou shalt have no other gods before me.

97. And Hebrews 10:25 says,

25 Not forsaking the assembling of ourselves together, as the manner of some is; but exhorting one another: and so much the more, as ye see the day approaching.

98. Would you feel that your partner had forsaken the relationship and the sanctity of it if they had sex with someone else, even just for one evening? Remember, they only paused your relationship and returned home to you afterward, claiming they did not forsake it.

99. It is clear that while he or she was in the hotel room with the other person (anywhere from an hour to six hours), they interrupted the relationship for that time,

even though they claimed not to have forsaken it. If that would make you feel bad and angry, consider how God feels when he says to put him first and have no other God before him, but you choose to miss church to vacation or any other reason!

100. Again, Matthew 5:48 says,

48 Be ye therefore perfect, even as your Father which is in heaven is perfect.

101. Tell me exactly which service God missed!

Nail in a Sure Place
102. Any time you do not attend church, you must describe it as missing church. Every time God met with people in the Bible, they called it church or a gathering. When people get mad and leave, the first thing they attack is attending church regularly; the second is they will decrease their offering amount; and thirdly, they disrespect the ministry or the body of Christ.

103. When you miss, you do not say you mistered; you say, "Miss (Eve)." People call the day before Christmas - Christmas Eve, not Christmas Adam, and they call the day before the New Year - New Year's Eve, not New Year's Adam.

104. Hebrews 13:5 says,

5 Let your conversation be without covetousness; and be content with such things as ye have: for he hath said, I will never leave thee, nor forsake thee.

178

105.   Some will forsake attending church once or twice, but God said he would not forsake you, so we have assurance knowing he will never have to forsake us because he forsook Jesus for us.

106.   Matthew 27:46 says,

46 And about the ninth hour Jesus cried with a loud voice, saying, Eli, Eli, lama sabachthani? that is to say, My God, my God, <u>why hast thou forsaken me</u>?

107.   Knowing us, he forsook Jesus so he would not have to forsake us; you should not look for reasons to forsake the assembling of yourself together because God forsook his son so he would not have to forsake you. You may be unable to say, "I will never leave or forsake the church," but God said, "I will never leave or forsake you." Think about that! We all deserve to have God forsake us.

108.   Deuteronomy 31:6 says,

6 Be strong and of a good courage, fear not, nor be afraid of them: for the Lord thy God, he it is that doth go with thee; he will not fail thee, nor forsake thee.

109.   God will not take a day off.

110.   Deuteronomy 31:8 says,

8 And the Lord, he it is that doth go before thee; he will be with thee, he will not fail thee, neither forsake thee: fear not, neither be dismayed.

179

111.   He told us not to forsake the assembling and said he would not forsake us either, so if we are bone of his bone and flesh of his flesh, we cannot forsake, and neither can God because it is not in us!

112.   Joshua 1:5 says,

5 There shall not any man be able to stand before thee all the days of thy life: as I was with Moses, so I will be with thee: I will not fail thee, nor forsake thee.

113.   God will not pause, interrupt, or miss; even if you think he is not there, he is because God said he would not forsake you.

114.   Jesus said in Matthew 28:20,

20 Teaching them to observe all things whatsoever I have commanded you: and, lo, I am with you alway, even unto the end of the world. Amen.

115.   Jesus did not say, "I am with you always" because "always" gives some wiggling room; he said, "I am with you alway." He will never leave or forsake you. I am driving the nail into a sure place.

116.   Deuteronomy 4:31 says,

31 (For the Lord thy God is a merciful God;) he will not forsake thee, neither destroy thee, nor forget the covenant of thy fathers which he sware unto them.

117.   And Deuteronomy 12:19 says,

19 Take heed to thyself that thou forsake not the Levite as long as thou livest upon the earth.

118.   Not only are you to not forsake the assembling of yourself, but you should also not forsake the man of God. You should stand by his side and hold his arms up, even for a weekend.

119.   Deuteronomy 14:27 says,

27 And the Levite that is within thy gates; thou shalt not forsake him; for he hath no part nor inheritance with thee.

120.   You should not forsake the man of God; do not take a pause.

121.   1 Samuel 12:22 says,

22 For the Lord will not forsake his people for his great name's sake: because it hath pleased the Lord to make you his people.

122.   God will not forsake his people because he forsook Jesus for us. It pleased God to make us his people, so why would you disrespect him? Why would you say, "Well, I need a vacation." Do you need a vacation more than you need to make love with God, who did everything for you?

123.   1 Chronicles 28:20 says,

20 And David said to Solomon his son, Be strong and of good courage, and do it: fear not, nor be dismayed: for the Lord God, even my God, will be with thee; he will not fail thee, nor forsake thee, until thou hast finished all the work for the service of the house of the Lord.

181

124.   Gather in God's house!

125.   Nehemiah 10:39 says,

39 For the children of Israel and the children of Levi shall bring the offering of the corn, of the new wine, and the oil, unto the chambers, where are the vessels of the sanctuary, and the priests that minister, and the porters, and the singers: and we will not forsake the house of our God.

126.   They said, "We will not forsake the house of our God!"

127.   Solomon said in 1 Kings 8:57,

57 The Lord our God be with us, as he was with our fathers: let him not leave us, nor forsake us:

128.   Solomon, God has answered your prayer.

129.   David said in Psalms 27:9,

9 Hide not thy face far from me; put not thy servant away in anger: thou hast been my help; leave me not, neither forsake me, O God of my salvation.

130.   I present God to you face to face, so if you miss a service, you have hidden your face from him. David does not have to worry because God will not forsake him.

131.   Again, Hebrews 13:5 says,

5 Let your conversation be without covetousness; and be content with such things as ye have: for he hath said, I will never leave thee, nor forsake thee.

132.　When God told us not to forsake the assembling in Hebrews 10:25, he did not think it was a big deal because we are bone of his bone and flesh of his flesh.

133.　1 Corinthians 2:16 says,

16 For who hath known the mind of the Lord, that he may instruct him? But we have the mind of Christ.

134.　He will not forsake us because he believes we will not forsake him. He put Hebrews 10:25 in the Bible because we are alike, but in case a knothead read it and did not understand, he put Hebrews 10:26 behind it to say, "If you sin willfully…."

135.　Millions claim to be Christian, but Hebrews 10:26 will put them in the Lake of Fire, not because of any fleshly sin like drunkenness, adultery, or gambling, but for not assembling themselves together. By missing church, they do to God what he said he would not do to them!

136.　Which service did God miss? Did snow prevent him? Did rain prevent him? Did death prevent him? No! Of course, as humans, we cannot circumvent death or illnesses that put us in a hospital, but you can fight through a snowstorm to attend church; you should try to get there.

137.   Atom means a moment of time or the twinkling of an eye, so if you miss one service, you miss the twinkling of an eye. If you miss one service, you miss an atom of time, a moment of time; God will not hold you accountable if you cannot attend church due to an illness or death.

138.   Someone may say, "I have to work." You do not have to work that job if it keeps you from attending church. Some ministers teach that if you miss church to work, you have not sinned because the Bible says that if you do not work, you do not eat. Again, you do not need to work at a job that will prevent you from assembling yourself together.   Some in my congregations gave up jobs to attend church and now have better ones than before.

139.   Hebrews 13:5 says,

5 Let your conversation be without covetousness; and be content with such things as ye have: for he hath said, I will never leave thee, nor forsake thee.

140.   If you plan to be perfect like God, you must attend church! He said he would never forsake us. Which service did he miss? If you have the mind of Christ, you will not miss a church service!

141.   Therefore, I end this book by using these scriptures:

142.   John 13:15 says,

15 For I have given you an example, that ye should do as I have done to you.

143.   Matthew 5:48 says,

48 Be ye therefore perfect, even as your Father which is in heaven is perfect.

How many services do you think that God misses? Amen.

References

1. PCStudy Bible, Electronic Database. 1996 Biblesoft
2. Ibid.
3. Roget's New Millennium™ Thesaurus, First Edition v 1.3.1, Copyright © 2007, by Lexico Publishing Group, LLC. www.dictionary.com
4. PCStudy Bible, Electronic Database. 1996 Biblesoft

Family Budget

1. God's work ⬅
2. Food
3. Clothing
4. Family
5. Father
6. Mother
7. Children
8. Possessions
9. Job
10. Career

Put God's work first on your list!

Forsake Synonyms

From Pastor Fulcher's Personal Notes:
According to Brown Driver & Briggs the definition of the word **forsake** is,

OT:5800
azab —

1	to leave, to loose, to forsake
a	Qal to leave
1	to depart from, to leave behind, to leave, to let alone
2	to leave, to abandon, to forsake, to neglect, to apostatize
3	to let loose, to set free, to let go, to free
b	Niphal
1	to be left to
2	to be forsaken
c	Pual to be deserted
2	to restore, to repair
	Qal to repair

from The Online Bible Thayer's Greek Lexicon and Brown Driver & Briggs Hebrew Lexicon, Copyright © 1993, Woodside Bible Fellowship, Ontario, Canada. Licensed from the Institute for Creation Research.

According to Strong's the definition of the word **forsake** is,

OT:7503

raphah raw-faw'; a primitive root; to slacken in many applications, literal or figurative:
KJV - abate, cease, consume, draw [toward evening], fail, be faint, be wax feeble, forsake, idle, leave, let alone go, down, be slack, stay, be still, be slothful, be weak -en. See

Biblesoft's New Exhaustive Strong's Numbers and Concordance with Expanded Greek-Hebrew Dictionary. Copyright © 1994, 2003 Biblesoft, Inc. and International Bible Translators, Inc.

According to Brown Driver & Briggs the definition of the word **forsake** is,

OT:7495

rapha' or raphah —

to heal, to make healthful

a	Qal to heal
1	of God
2	a healer, a physician of men
3	used of the hurts of nations involving restored favor figurative
4	used of individual distresses figurative
b	Niphal to be healed
1	literal used of persons
2	used of water, pottery

188

3	used of national hurts figurative
4	used of personal distress figurative
c	Piel to heal
1	literal
2	used of national defects or hurts figurative
d	Hithpael in order to get healed infinitive

from The Online Bible Thayer's Greek Lexicon and Brown Driver & Briggs Hebrew Lexicon, Copyright © 1993, Woodside Bible Fellowship, Ontario, Canada. Licensed from the Institute for Creation Research.

According to Thayer's Greek Lexicon the definition of the word **forsake** is,

NT:1459

the Septuagint LXX for `aazab;

1. to <u>abandon</u>, desert en equivalent to en tini, in some place or condition, i. e. to leave in straits, leave helpless, colloquial, leave in the lurch:
tina, Matt 27:46 and Mark 15:34 from Ps. 21:2 22:2; Heb 13:5; passive 2 Cor 4:9;

from Thayer's Greek Lexicon, Electronic Database. Copyright c 2000 by Biblesoft

The following are synonyms for the words forsaking, abandon, and abandonment.

Forsaking

Main Entry   defection

Definition   break

Synonyms   <u>abandon</u>, <u>be unfaithful</u>, betray, change, desert, forsake, renege, repudiate, retract, return, revert.

Abandon

Main Entry   Betray

Definition   deceive

Synonyms   <u>abandon</u>, <u>be unfaithful</u>, bluff, break faith, break promise, break trust, break with, commit treason, cross, deceive, deliver up, delude, desert, double-cross, finger, forsake, inform against, inform on, jilt, knife, let down, mislead, sell, sell out, take in, trick, turn in, turn informer.

Main Entry   break

Definition   stop

Synonyms   <u>abandon</u>, cut, discontinue, give up, <u>interrupt</u>, <u>pause</u>, rest, suspend.

Main Entry   drop out

Definition   stop

Synonyms   <u>abandon</u>, back out, cease, forsake, give notice, give up, leave, quit, renege, retreat, withdraw.

Main Entry   Evacuate

Definition   empty

Synonyms   <u>abandon</u>, bail out, clear, cut out, decamp, depart, desert, discharge, displace, eject, expel, forsake, hightail, leave, move out, pack up, pull out, quit, relinquish, remove, skidoo, vacate, withdraw.

Main Entry   depart

Definition   leave

Synonyms   <u>abandon</u>, abdicate, absent, beat it, blast off, blow, cut out, decamp, desert, disappear, emigrate, escape, evacuate, exit, get away, git, go, go away, go forth, make feet, march out, migrate, move on, move out, part, perish, pull out, quit, remove, retire, sally forth, say goodbye, scram, secede, set forth, shove off, slip away, split, start, start out, take leave, tergiversate, troop, vacate, vanish, withdraw.

Main Entry   desist

Definition   stop

Synonyms   <u>abandon</u>, abstain, avoid, break off, cease, deval, discontinue, end, forbear, give over, give up, halt, knock off, leave off, not do, <u>pause</u>, quit, refrain, relinquish, resign, surcease, <u>suspend</u>, yield.

Main Entry   discontinue

Definition   prevent

Synonyms   <u>abandon</u>, bag it, blow off, break off, cease, close, desist, disconnect, disjoin, dissever, disunite, drop, end, finish, give over, give up, halt, interpose, <u>interrupt</u>, intervene, kill, knock off, leave off, part, <u>pause</u>, quit, refrain from, scrub, separate, stop, surcease, <u>suspend</u>, terminate.

Main Entry   cop out

Definition   quit

Synonyms   <u>abandon</u>, alibi, back down, back off, back out, backpedal, desert, dodge, excuse, rationalize, renege, renounce, revoke, <u>skip</u>, use pretext, welsh, withdraw.

Main Entry   defect

Definition   back out

Synonyms   abandon, abscond, <u>apostatize</u>, break faith, break from, change sides, depart, desert, forsake, go, go over, leave, pull out, quit, rat, rebel, reject, renege, renounce, revolt, run out, sell out, spurn, tergiversate, tergiverse, turn, turn coat, withdraw.

Main Entry   go back

Definition   break

Synonyms   abandon, <u>be unfaithful</u>, betray, change, desert, forsake, renege, repudiate, retract, return, revert.

Main Entry   jump

Definition   <u>abandonment</u>

Synonyms   abandon, cancel, clear out, cover, cross out, digress, evade, leave, <u>miss</u>, nullify, omit, overshoot, pass over, skip, switch

Main Entry   license

Definition   indulgence

Synonyms   abandon, anarchy, animalism, arrogance, audacity, boldness, complacency, debauchery, disorder, effrontery, excess, forwardness, gluttony, immoderation, impropriety, irresponsibility, lawlessness, laxity, looseness, presumptuousness, prodigality, profligacy, refractoriness, relaxation, relaxedness, sauciness, self-indulgence, sensuality, <u>slackness</u>, temerity, unrestraint, unruliness, wantonness, wildness.

Abandonment

Main Entry   departure

Definition   leaving

Synonyms   abandonment, adieu, conge, decampment, departing, desertion, egress, egression, embarkation, emigration, escape, evacuation, exit, exodus, expatriation, farewell, flight, getaway, going, going away, goodbye, hegira, leave-taking, migration, parting, passage, powder, quitting, recession, removal, retirement, retreat, sailing, separation, setting forth, setting out, stampede, starting, take-off, taking leave, taking off, <u>vacation</u>, vanishing act, walkout, withdrawal, withdrawing.

Main Entry   dissipation

Definition   wantonness

Synonyms   abandonment, debauchery, dissoluteness, dissolution, drunkenness, evil, excess, extravagance, free-living, hell-bent, high living, indulgence, intemperance, lavishness, prodigality, profligacy, <u>self-gratification</u>, squandering, waste.

Main Entry   waiver

Definition   giving up

Synonyms   abandonment, abdication, disclaimer, forgoing, letting go, postponement, refusal, rejection, relinquishment, remission, renunciation, reservation, resignation, <u>setting aside</u>, surrender, tabling.

Main Entry   ditch

Definition   get rid of

Synonyms   abandonment, cashier, chuck, desert,
discard, dispose of, drop, dump, forsake, jettison, junk,
leave, reject, scrap, throw away, throw out.

Main Entry   give in

Definition   admit defeat

Synonyms   abandon, back down, bail out, bow out,
buckle under, capitulate, cave in, cease, cede, chicken
out, collapse, comply, concede, cry uncle, cut out,
desist, despair, drop, fold, forswear, give up, hand
over, leave off, pull out, quit, relinquish, resign, stop,
submit, surrender, waive, yield.

Source   Roget's New Millennium™ Thesaurus, First Edition v 1.3.1
Copyright © 2007 by Lexico Pulishing Group, LLC. All rights reserved.

Booklets:

Blood On the doorpost
Decoy Revival
Don't Be Called Reverend
Foolish Virgins
Pharisee Religion
Office Of the Ministry
Serpent Seed and The Sin of Ham
The Bottomless Pit
The Justification Covenant
The Origin of Steeples
The Revealing of Christ (In a parable)
The Truth About Easter
The Truth About Valentine's Day
Trial of Jealousy
What About the Cross?
What Are the Gates of Hell
What Is the Holy Ghost
Who Is Lucifer

Books:

Communion / Foot Washing / Water Baptism
Paganism In Christianity
Reversing Paradise
The Truth About Christmas
The Truth About Halloween
Unclean Period

Write to the following address for current prices:

Dr. E. C. Fulcher, Jr.
Po Box 973
Abingdon, Md. 21009

Visit our website and explore our Library; browse all the books, Present Testament Articles, Weekly Newsletters, Global Shortwave Club Newsletters and "My Road to Truth" Articles.

www.truthhouse.org